Praise for *The Boomer Burden*

"Maybe the most practical book I've read in years. This should be on every baby boomer's must-read list. A sound, down-to-earth, well-written manual for one of the most difficult subjects to discuss with your parents . . . and I'm including the birds and the bees lecture decades earlier."

— BOB HAMER
Veteran FBI Agent and Author,
The Last Undercover

"Julie has created a masterpiece on how to help your parents and yourself deal with several very stressful and emotionally charged issues. Julie's storytelling of examples garnered over years of working with families guides her readers and creates scenarios that they can easily relate to in their own lives. As a certified financial planner, all of my clients will be given a copy of Julie's book as required reading. This book is the most comprehensive and thoughtful work on a difficult and complex aspect of life. A must-read for boomers dealing with everybody's stuff!"

— ADOLPHUS W. DUNN III
CPA, CFP, AEP

"As a personal family lawyer, I've had to deal with much of the fallout over the issues Julie addresses in her book. Most of us will, at some point, have to care for our parents and their stuff, and it can be an overwhelming burden, but with the information Julie shares, we can avoid many of the potential problems. Julie's book provides fantastic insight that helps us anticipate difficulties and find workable solutions."

— ALEXIS MARTIN NEELY
America's Personal Family Lawyer,
www.PersonalFamilyLawyer.com;
and Author, *Wear Clean Underwear:
A Fast, Fun, Friendly—and
Essential—Guide to Legal
Planning for Busy Parents*

"It was sharp-witted Benjamin Franklin who observed that in this world nothing is certain but death and taxes. Now, through the wisdom of Julie Hall, you can add a third: dealing with the aftermath of your parent's death. *The Boomer Burden* is an exceptionally well-written and wise book. Both parents and adult children need the wake-up call that Julie so deftly and confidently offers. It speaks with the voice of experience and comforts with a deep empathy for this painful period of life. Mostly, it offers reassurance that at a time of deep grief, adult children can and *must* be prepared for life's third certainty. There is no doubt in my mind that this book is essential reading for both older parents and adult children—and it will be especially beneficial if they read it together."

— ARCHIBALD D. HART, PhD, FPPR
Clinical Psychologist; Senior Professor
of Psychology and Dean Emeritus,
Graduate School of Psychology, Fuller
Theological Seminary; and Author,
Thrilled to Death

"*The Boomer Burden* is an engaging and comprehensive treatment of the end-of-life dynamics between aging parents and aging children. While this book is complete with helpful summaries and checklists, the author also uses engaging anecdotes that exemplify the importance of the process. I will recommend *The Boomer Burden* to my estate planning clients."

— MALVERN KING
Partner, Pulley, Watson,
King & Lischer, P.A., Attorneys at Law

Boomer *the* Burden

Boomer *the* Burden

DEALING WITH YOUR PARENTS' LIFETIME ACCUMULATION OF STUFF

Julie Hall

THE ESTATE LADY®

THOMAS NELSON
Since 1798

NASHVILLE DALLAS MEXICO CITY RIO DE JANEIRO BEIJING

Published in Nashville, Tennessee, by Thomas Nelson. Thomas Nelson is a registered trademark of Thomas Nelson, Inc.

Published in association with Rosenbaum & Associates Literary Agency, Brentwood, Tennessee.

Thomas Nelson, Inc., titles may be purchased in bulk for educational, business, fund-raising, or sales promotional use. For information, please e-mail SpecialMarkets@ThomasNelson.com.

The Estate Lady® is a registered trademark of Julie Hall. Used with permission. All rights reserved.

Scripture quotations marked NKJV are taken from the New King James Version®. ©1982 by Thomas Nelson, Inc. Used by permission. All rights reserved.

Scripture quotations marked KJV are taken from the King James Version of the Bible.

This publication is intended to provide authoritative information in regard to the subject matter covered. It is purchased with the understanding that estate laws may vary from state to state and that the publisher is not giving advice nor rendering legal, accounting, or other professional services. If you require legal advice or other expert assistance, you should seek the services of a competent professional in that field.

Library of Congress Cataloging-in-Publication Data

Hall, Julie.
    The boomer burden : dealing with your parents' lifetime accumulation of stuff / Julie Hall.
      p. cm.
    Includes bibliographical references.
    ISBN 978-0-7852-2825-7 (pbk.)
    1. Administration of estates. 2. Estate planning. 3. Baby boom generation. 4. Aging parents. I. Title.
HG4319.H35 2008
646.7'8—dc22   2008003174

Printed in the United States of America

08 09 10 11 12 RRD 5 4 3 2 1

For all my clients—past, present, and future.

If it weren't for you and your families,
I would never have become The Estate Lady®.

Thank you for sharing your lives so I could learn
how to serve you in a greater capacity.

Contents

Contents

Acknowledgments

Have you ever heard the saying, "When the student is ready, the teacher appears?" These are my teachers, to whom I offer my deepest heartfelt appreciation for listening to my stories, understanding the great need for this book, helping me open doors with unbelievable speed, and answering more questions than a roomful of preschoolers could possibly ask.

To my literary agent, Bucky Rosenbaum, and your wife, Joann: Our meeting was not by chance. Helping you and your in-laws during your personal time of need was a privilege. Thank you for seeing the importance of this work and helping me get this book published so my experience can serve others. Thank you for planting the seed.

To my editorial consultant, Lyn Cryderman, who listens more attentively than anyone I know: I thank you for your unwavering support and understanding of how to get what's inside my brain out on paper. I thank you for your gentle guidance along the way. Having already been where the reader is headed, you were invaluable in helping me get the message out there.

To my acquisitions editor, Debbie Wickwire: Your excitement from the moment you saw the proposal has been contagious! Your belief in the critical need for this book and in me is more appreciated than you will ever know.

To my publisher, Joey Paul: Thank you for your kindness and understanding that there is a tremendous need for this book. I am grateful to you and to everyone at Thomas Nelson for this opportunity.

To my editors, Jennifer Stair and Paula Major: Thank you for bringing this book together and making it shine! Your input and changes brought out the best it has to offer.

To Larry Carpenter, Scott Harris, Jennifer Womble, and Beth Hood: a world-class marketing team that has my sincerest heartfelt gratitude for launching *The Boomer Burden.*

To Jonathan Frank, estate planning attorney in Charlotte, North Carolina: Thank you for your patient assistance and contribution to the cause. You helped us understand the necessary legal documents and the need to be prepared for the inevitable.

To my colleague Jennifer Szakaly, MA, geriatric care manager of CareGiving Corner in Charlotte, North Carolina: Your input and guidance with the early chapters is greatly appreciated, since you work with seniors and their children every day. Thank you for all your good advice.

To Joseph Henninger, Danica Little, and Brenda Solomon at Wishart Norris Henninger & Pittman, P.A. in Burlington and Charlotte, North Carolina: I thank you all for your sound advice and willingness to let me ask so many questions.

To Fran Mathay, Polly Furr, and Rosalie Spaniel: Thank all of you for helping me launch this book, listening to my ideas, and getting me started in the right direction!

To Patrice, my assistant and my right-hand lady: No one will ever know what we have seen, experienced, and lived through with our clients. And no one will probably ever see human nature the way we do. Thanks for making the often unbearable situations more bearable with your wit, songs, stories, and life theories.

I have also been very blessed with a supportive and caring family, without whom this book would never have been written.

To my parents, Anne and Bill: Your sure and steadfast ways have instilled in me a sense of great responsibility and courage to reach out and serve many. Thank you for showing me the right path and for making me understand that nothing worthwhile in life comes easily. While the gift of speech has always come easily for me, saying "I love you" could never be enough.

Acknowledgments

To my husband, Bob: You are my own personal Rock of Gibraltar. Through all my anxious moments, late-night book ideas, heart-wrenching client situations, quandaries of raising an adolescent, and my chronic entrepreneurial streak, you remain as steady as the North Star. Your faithful love and encouragement is like a beacon lighting my way. You are, and always will be, my only love.

To my daughter, Eva: You are among the most patient of my supporters. When I am home alone with my thoughts, all I have to do is think of "my bony little giraffe." Thank you for your steady understanding and for allowing me to fulfill a dream. You are the reason my heart beats.

Author's Note

This book will guide you through a process I've walked with thousands of clients—settling and cleaning out your parents' estate after they pass away. I know this is a difficult subject, and some of the details discussed in these chapters are not pleasant. After all, no one wants to think about their parents' eventual deaths! But please stick with me because the information and insights I reveal to you in this book, if applied, will keep you from making costly mistakes and heart-wrenching oversights that would be truly depressing. Based on my many years of experience in estate dissolution, I will teach you practical, effective steps you can take to distribute your parents' assets in a way that honors them and promotes family harmony for generations to come.

If you are reading this because you have an immediate need, then you are feeling an overwhelming burden—the boomer burden. You are not alone. You are one of thousands of men and women in the baby boomer generation dealing with your parents' lifetime of accumulation. Even if your parents are still in relatively good health, the best way to deal with this inevitable situation is to act now to gain the knowledge and assistance you need to walk through this process in a way that would make your parents proud.

This book will provide you with the trustworthy counsel you need when facing the monumental task of walking your parents through their final days and then settling their estate. If you read this book from beginning to end, you will see that there is hope at the end of this journey. It is my desire that the experiences and insights packed in these pages will touch your heart as they have mine.

A Special Note to Older Parents

I wrote this book specifically for your adult children because I care about you and your family. Some of the advice I offer them could alarm you. For example, I address the delicate subject of what your children should do if you become unable to live on your own but, understandably, do not want to leave your home. This presents a difficult dilemma to your children. On the one hand, they respect your wishes to stay in your home; but on the other hand, they want you to be safe and dread the thought of you injuring yourself, or worse. I also advise your children what to do if you become medically incapacitated and how to protect you from shysters who prey on senior citizens.

Whether you agree with my advice in this book or not, you can prevent your children from having to struggle with those kinds of decisions. In fact, I wish you would. For starters, make sure you have made out a will, even if you are in great health and expect to stay that way for a long time. If you already have made out a will, take the time right now to review it and update it if necessary. This is one of the best gifts you can give your children. It can prevent many of the problems I address in this book.

The next thing you can do to avoid unnecessary misunderstandings as you grow older is to sit down with your children and have a frank discussion about some things that are not easy to talk about:

- What should your children do if you and your spouse become seriously incapacitated and can no longer manage in your own home?
- What measures should your children request from medical professionals if you become incapacitated and your physician does not think you will recover?
- Who should make important decisions for you if you are diagnosed with Alzheimer's and experience confusion and memory loss?

- What specific requests do you have for your funeral or other last wishes?

No one wants to think about these things, but at some point we all have to make these decisions; if we don't, someone else will do it for us. Often those choices are not what you would have wanted. Please don't wait another day to have this conversation with your children. Do it now while you can. Or if your children come to you about these issues, as I recommend in this book, receive them warmly and ease their fears about asking these kinds of questions.

Finally, begin going through your home and make some decisions about the things you don't need that may have piled up over the years. This will accomplish two things. First, your children won't have to do it later. Second, you'll lighten my load because I earn my living by clearing the clutter out of homes like yours. But that's okay. I'm no spring chicken anymore, and my back will thank you!

Though this book is written primarily to your adult children, I have included special sidebars throughout the chapters to highlight information specifically for you, the parents. Please take time to read these sidebars carefully and then take action now to take care of these important details—that will be a treasured gift to all your children.

I went into the estate business because I have a very special compassion for older adults. I have seen how they are preyed upon by dishonest people who pose as "helpers." And I have wept with elderly parents like you who share your fears about children fighting over family heirlooms. So if you read anything in this book that offends you, I am truly sorry. If what I write makes you angry, turn that into action and start talking to your children about what *you* want. Problems arise when parents and children do not have open communication.

More than anything, I want you to have complete control over the rest of your life. You not only deserve it, but it's also your legal right.

Introduction

Leaving Behind More Than Memories

Every day approximately forty-eight hundred baby boomers become middle-aged orphans.[1] Their elderly parents, members of what has been called the Greatest Generation, have passed away, leaving behind a lot more than just memories. According to Boston College economist John J. Havens, parents of boomers will leave assets of as much as $41 trillion to their adult children.[2] And that's not counting the boxes and piles of stuff that are left behind. However, the vast majority of those who find themselves on the receiving end of this windfall are totally unprepared for the challenge awaiting them as they and their siblings attempt to divide the wealth and benefit from the legacy their parents left them.

I should know. For the past seventeen years, I have assisted thousands of people through the process of managing and dividing the belongings of their parents' estate. It sounds like a dream job, right? I walk through lovely older homes with the surviving adult children, assessing the value of furniture, china, jewelry, appliances, and electronics. Sometimes I run across a valuable surprise, like the time a family was about to donate a pair of vases to charity until I did a little research and sold them for $57,500! Then I watch the family members take turns selecting pieces they want to keep and donating the leftovers.

You would think helping families settle the estates of their parents would be a walk in the park. It's actually more like refereeing a heavyweight boxing match, complete with low blows and knockout punches. And then you have to clean up after the fight. I've seen it all, and most of it is not very pretty. Take, for example, the time when one sister accused the other of stealing valuables from their parents' basement as the rest of the family stood vigil beside their dying father's bedside *upstairs*! One time I had to inform survivors that the inheritance they had hoped to receive no longer existed because their aged and confused mother had been scammed several times in the years leading up to her death. Many times siblings end up fighting one another in court because their deceased parents did not prepare a will or share their estate plans and final wishes with the children. Most of these issues are *preventable*, as you will see throughout this book.

You might think I'm exaggerating or that these are extreme examples, but sadly, these kinds of situations are the norm. Fewer than 20 percent of the estates I've handled have gone smoothly. The rest have been filled with confusion, anger, jealousy, huge legal expenses, and broken relationships between surviving siblings.

I am almost certain that as you read this, you see yourself and your family in the 20 percent group, and I sincerely hope you are. You're probably a very nice person in a close family where everyone gets along well and enjoys one another's company. Most of the people I work with are also nice people with lovely families. They have successful careers and generally don't need the wealth that is left behind by their parents. They share memories of warm family traditions, holiday gatherings, weddings, births, graduations, and first Communions. From all appearances, these are siblings who truly get along with one another. But when the last parent dies and they are faced with a lifetime of accumulation and a potential windfall, something happens to these good families, and the results are often unsettling. The familial glue begins to dissolve.

It doesn't have to be that way for you, and that's why I'm writing this book. I really believe that most people want to do the right thing; but in the stress and emotional turmoil that come with the loss of a parent or both parents, we often do things we later regret.

A Daunting Task

For one thing, the sheer amount of work involved in closing your parents' estate is daunting. I recall the time I walked into the family home with a middle-aged woman whose mom had just passed away. She looked at the piles of stuff tucked into closets, the attic, garage, and basement and was stunned. Thinking she was still grieving, I left her alone for a few minutes while I toured the house. When I came back to her in the living room, she appeared to be angry.

"Is there something wrong?" I asked.

"Yes, as a matter of fact, there is!" she snapped. "I *knew* this would happen. For years I tried to get Mom to sort through all of this stuff, and she refused. Now I'm stuck with it, and my brother won't lift a finger to help me. This is so overwhelming. There's no way I'm going to get through this."

I tried to reassure her as I began going over the usual questions I ask when I'm hired to help liquidate estates, but it got worse as we discovered there were no records of bank accounts, insurance policies, or investments. From the piles of unopened mail, it was clear that bills hadn't been paid in several months, and the daughter didn't have a clue as to whether a will even existed. The more questions I asked, the angrier she became until at one point she blurted out, "I can't do this! Just do whatever you have to do, and send me the bill." And with that, she walked out of the house she grew up in as a child, got in her car, and drove away, leaving me with the keys and instructions to deal with the entire estate.

I knew this woman fairly well and had always thought of her as a real sweetheart. And I still do because I have seen how devastating it is to lose a parent and then to face the reality that no one had prepared for this eventuality. I see this sad situation over and over again in families all across America. I call it *the boomer burden.* If a family has not adequately prepared for the inevitable loss of their parents, the grief at the funeral will quickly turn into a nightmare.

For those who are unprepared for this event, the legal technicalities and process of cleaning out the parents' estate can drag on for months and sometimes years. Adult children who live in another city, or even across the country, require a significant amount of travel and an extended absence from work and family to sort through these details. I have known people who actually lost their jobs because this process took such a long time.

But if you follow the procedures and insights I describe in this book, you can clear out your parents' estate in seven to ten days. The tools I give you in these chapters will equip you to complete this difficult process much more peacefully and efficiently.

The process of settling an estate can often drag on for many months for various reasons:

- Boomers are often geographically remote from their parents, requiring extensive travel and time away from work and family.

- Adult children who have moved to another city or state may not know the local resources for handling the estate and have to research this information.

- Boomers whose parents did not leave a will may have to wait for the state to divide their parents' assets.

- Boomers whose parents did not leave specific information about bank accounts, insurance policies, and so on have to search for this information.

- Many boomers don't know the value of their parents' personal property and aren't sure how to find out.

- Feuding between siblings often prolongs and complicates the process of asset distribution.

The Time Is Now!

Ideally, when you bought this book, your parents were both living, in reasonably good health, and still mentally sharp. If that is the case, and you apply everything you learn in this book, the eventual task of liquidating your parents' estate will go smoothly. I will coach you on how to have "that conversation" with your parents, how to involve your siblings, and how to avoid some of the problems that come up along the way. In appendix A, you will find a helpful checklist of the things that need to be done now and at the time of loss.

More than likely, though, you bought this book because you're in the middle of a crisis. Perhaps it has become clear to you and your siblings that your parents can no longer live in their home. Or one of your parents is deceased and the other one is seriously ill, perhaps even incapacitated. Most of us tend to avoid dealing with the issue of our parents' passing until it happens, so if this describes you, you're in good company. The information in this book will help you reduce the stress and anxiety that come with dealing with these issues.

Note to Parents

A crisis can occur at any time for anybody. As you will see in the coming pages, thinking out your plans and making decisions is vital for your children's well-being and peace of mind. They often second-guess their decisions and wish they had more direction from you. If you offer your children specific directions about your last wishes and discuss these plans, backed up with legal documents, then your children will thank you and respect you for easing their load at a time of crisis.

I would love to think this book could also fall into the hands of your parents if they are still living. While I have found that these wonderful members of our Greatest Generation generally avoid talking about things such as death, wills, and the location of their bank accounts, this book could help them take control of their final years and give them comfort in knowing their children will not have to go through a distressing ordeal when they pass away. I have seen firsthand what happens when the elderly parents take the lead in making sure everything is in order, and it is so much easier on everyone when that happens.

By the way, you will notice I use the word *estate* throughout this book. For some people, this word conjures up images of ornate mansions on beautifully landscaped rolling acres. *Estate* is simply a term used to describe a person's home and belongings. Your parents' estate could be a mobile home on a small rented lot, a three-bedroom ranch house in the suburbs, or, yes, an ornate mansion on several acres. Your parents' estate includes everything they leave behind—home, furniture, automobile, pension, investments, knickknacks, and so on.

Note to Parents

When the parent(s) takes the lead, the children are much calmer through the entire process. The faces of your children are relaxed and bear an expression of appreciation for making plans ahead of time. I have heard many children say, "I am so glad Mom and Dad had all of their affairs in order. That relieved us of so much pressure and guessing."

Becoming Your Advocate

You might wonder how I got into this line of work. It happened almost by accident. I actually started out in the pharmaceutical industry. As a hobby, I began collecting antiques and soon discovered I had a knack for picking out the valuable pieces from the junk. A personal property appraiser told me he thought I had a real gift and offered me a job. I thought, *Why not?* and began a successful new career in the antiques business. And then I met Wilma.

Wilma was 103 years old when I met her. Spry and feisty, she wanted me to help her clear out some of her belongings as she was selling her home. Wilma and I walked through her home one afternoon, stopping at memorable pieces as she shared fascinating stories behind each item. Wilma had lived in Germany for eighty years, and it was clear she had numerous items of value—Meissen figurines, early-twentieth-century art glass, antique Lalique pieces, and elegant nineteenth-century inlaid French furniture. Her home was a small museum filled with treasures of every size and description. I promised to return in a few days and help her sell the items.

When I entered Wilma's house a few days later, I couldn't believe my eyes. It was as if a small tornado had blown through the place. Her orderly home, once brimming with treasures, was in shambles. Each room was pillaged, leaving broken pieces behind. The new owners had "generously" offered to purchase the items of value and remove the rest. I discovered they offered only $5 for the figurines that were worth $500 to $900. The French furniture I estimated to be worth $20,000 was sold for only $500!

Wilma and I sat in the living room on the lone green velvet sofa as I tried to explain how she had been scammed by "people predators," a phrase I have coined for those who prey on the elderly. Although I could see the sadness in her eyes as we talked, she said something that convinced me I had a new calling: "It's a shame they got all those wonderful treasures for so little money, but where I'm going, I have no need for such things. I just don't want to leave a mess for anyone. I only wish we older people could have an estate lady like you when we face this."

Instantly I knew I had a new career direction—to educate and advocate for older adults and their children when the time comes for the elderly parents to part with their possessions. Wilma's comment even gave me the name for my new company: The Estate Lady.

While I may not be able to walk through your parents' home with you and crawl into attics or dig deep into closets, we can walk through this difficult process together. I have helped many clients with exactly the kinds of things you will face, and I assure you that you will get through this much easier if you allow this book to guide you along the way.

One

First Signs

You can't escape it—the sense of dread is hovering over everything you do. This is the pivotal moment in each boomer's life: you see your parents becoming more afflicted with age and fragility, and you are hit by a dizzying feeling of all the details about to land on your lap. I call this experience *the flying brick*, and it will strike you right between the eyes if you are not prepared. Suddenly you become all too aware of what your parents are doing—and *not* doing—such as eating well, paying bills, keeping up with the house, personal hygiene, and so on. Their behavior may be odd and troublesome. Their home is filled with stacks of clutter you have tried to get them to clear out for a decade. The kitchen cabinets are crammed with canned goods, most of them expired. The attic is filled with memories, but everything has rotted with the passage of time and exposure to the elements. All the bills and finances are out of order. You are beginning to see the writing on the wall.

I'd like to share with you a heart-wrenching story that still makes the hair on the back of my neck stand up when I think of it, and it caused me to write this book. Some of you will be able to relate to this experience, and others will be horrified by it. My hope in sharing my personal, real-life stories in this book is to move you into action, realizing what you can glean from these experiences.

The Crime Scene

Receiving a phone call from someone in crisis is common at my office, but when the phone rang one afternoon, and it was a colleague claiming an emergency, I knew the matter was very urgent.

My colleague said one of his clients, who was preparing to move to a safe environment for those afflicted with Alzheimer's, was at home alone when her neighbors—so-called friends—and a few antique dealers all decided to pay her a visit on the same afternoon. (Word spreads like wildfire any time an older adult begins downsizing an estate, and I caution you to pay close attention to this story so you can protect your loved ones.)

With a frantic tone in his voice, he urged me to drop what I was doing to visit his client. This elderly woman, suffering from Alzheimer's, was alone in her home, which was filled with many valuable possessions. Apparently several people, who had found out that she was moving into an assisted-living facility, came by to "purchase" all of her assets. My colleague had tried to get the dealers out of the house, but no one took him seriously. Knowing that I deal with this sort of thing daily and that I was only a short distance from the woman's home, he asked me to intervene quickly.

I had never met this elderly woman but knew I was being asked to take care of a very difficult situation. You see, these neighbors and friends and dealers were literally stripping her home of her lifelong heirlooms, possessions that were supposed to be passed down to her children after her death. But sadly, her children would never see those heirlooms again.

After arriving at the home and introducing myself to the elderly woman, I encouraged her to phone her daughter and son and allow me to speak with them. My colleague and I did not have her children's phone numbers, and the assisted-living facility could not give us that information for legal reasons. So our only hope was for this precious woman to give us their contact information. But her disease had progressed too far, and my efforts proved futile. There were nine friends and neighbors in her home, busily packing and wrapping valuable items, throwing money at her for things they were taking. In her advanced diseased state, she simply didn't know any better. But *they* did.

It didn't take long for my temper to flare, and I approached each friend and neighbor and dealer, pleading with them to pay her at least half of what these items were worth because her long-term care in the Alzheimer's facility would cost a tremendous amount annually. Again, my efforts proved futile. Not one of them acknowledged my presence. This went on and on. What I witnessed was like watching a vulture strip a bone—clean, fast, and leaving no evidence of what used to be. I watched in horror as all her beautiful possessions disappeared from her once-lovely home. The sterling flatware worth $2,000 went out the door for $20; the antique $1,000 desk was taken for $15; the antique French bronze mantel clock worth $2,500 walked out the door for $50; and other valuable antique furniture left for $10 and $20, never to return. How I wished her children could have been there to defend her. How I wished they would have known to expect exploitation in times of fragility!

The sensation of my heart sinking was almost more than I could take. But my work was not yet finished. Interestingly enough, when I approached these "vultures," they refused to look at me because they were well aware of what they were doing. In my disgust for what I had just witnessed, I angrily shouted, "How will any of you sleep tonight, knowing what you have done to this woman who cannot defend herself?"

Not one person looked up. No one even uttered a word. And no one dared to look me in the eyes. What they did, however, was wrap up these heirlooms even faster and shove them in their vehicles for a quick getaway.

Feeling totally helpless, I called a friend who is a sergeant on the police force. "Sergeant, here's the situation. Can I get anyone who's doing this on grand larceny? They are ripping this poor lady off." He asked me a number of questions, starting with, "Did she accept the money regardless of how little it was?" I replied, "Yes, but she does not have all her mental faculties."

"Can you prove it?" asked my police friend. Well, the elderly woman's deteriorating medical condition could have been proven, but it would have taken many months and going to court to do so.

The sergeant said, "Julie, we see this all the time. I know it's really hard to watch. There's nothing you can do about it because she willingly accepted the payment for these items. The kids left her alone in the house too long. I'm sorry, but there is *nothing you can do.*"

Those words changed the course of my life forever. I'm a professional in the estate industry who has seen virtually everything. Someone telling me "there's nothing you can do" was a lot like that flying brick—I just didn't see it coming. For me, the thought of not being able to do anything to help this poor woman was pure torture. Then it hit me: if this one woman could do nothing to help herself, and I wasn't there as her hired estate professional guarding her estate, imagine how many other senior adults are getting ripped off every hour of every day in every city? My head began to spin!

When I returned to my office, I closed the door and wept for what seemed like hours. Alone at my desk, the solitude invited deep thought. I wept for this woman with Alzheimer's, who had been grossly taken advantage of by unscrupulous people. I wept because I was totally helpless in the situation. Her children could not be reached, and I had no authority over her estate; all I had was my voice and anger, which didn't get me very far. And I wept because I knew thousands of people just like this woman were getting ripped off every single day. We are supposed to help one another, especially those who cannot help themselves. If you were in that woman's situation, wouldn't you want some kind person to look after you?

It took me quite a while to realize that my feelings of anger and outrage could be turned into a positive course of action. My new goal was to inspire boomer children to deal with their parents' estate and possessions with knowledge and peace of mind. And so this book was written just for you, a true labor of love with care and compassion for you and your family.

I know this story seems almost too awful to be true, but it really happened, and I see similar episodes of people preying on helpless older adults. But even if there are no predators involved, facing the inevitable decline of your parents can be just as heart wrenching. Maybe you can relate to Don and Mary's story.

Something You Don't Want to Think About

As Don backed the car out of the driveway of Mary's parents' home—the home Mary grew up in—they said little to each other. Mary felt the lump in her throat grow as she fought back tears, watching her mom wave from the wide front porch. She recalled the many mornings when her mom stood in that very spot and waved as Mary climbed onto the school bus waiting at the end of the driveway. Sometimes her mom would yell out, "Your lunch!" and then run back into the house to retrieve the brown bag she had just packed earlier with a healthy meal. *How different she is now,* Mary thought, recalling what had happened just moments ago.

Ever since her dad retired, these occasional trips to her hometown had been a joy. It was so good to see her dad enjoying his much-deserved retirement from the textile plant he managed, and Mary's kids loved sitting on the big front porch with Grandma as she told them stories about her own childhood and taught the girls how to weave garlands from the daisies she grew in her garden.

But a year ago Mary's dad had suffered a stroke, and the trips were harder to make. He had recovered well enough, even regaining most of the functions he'd lost, but it wasn't the same. Once a robust, gregarious man who golfed almost every day since he left the plant, he now spent most of his time watching television or sitting in his favorite chair by the window, paging through magazines or watching the traffic on the now-busy street in front of the house. Her mom did her best to cheer him up and keep him active, as the doctor told her she should do, but it was getting difficult for her to get around because of her knees.

Finally Mary spoke. "Maybe we should find someone to come in and do their laundry. Those stairs to the basement are just too much for Mom, and I noticed this time that both of them look like they're wearing the same clothes every day."

Her husband eased the car onto the freeway and then reached over to grab her hand. "Speaking of the basement, have you been down there lately? I went down to get a wrench from Dad's tool bench, and I could barely walk through all the stacks on the floor. There is stuff everywhere: magazines, cases of canning jars, coffee cans, cardboard boxes, mildewed books—piles of stuff that haven't been used in years. It's as if they tried sorting all their things and just gave up."

"Yeah, I wasn't going to say anything, but it's pretty bad. I asked Mom about it, and she acted like it was nothing. She even got a little testy with me, which just isn't like her."

They rode on in silence, passing shopping centers and strip malls and housing developments where cows once grazed.

Finally, Don spoke. "You know, Mary, they may need more than someone coming in to do the laundry. That little flare-up on the stove could have been a disaster if we hadn't been there. Your mom's still a great cook, but every now and then she just sort of zones out. Have you noticed that?"

Mary couldn't answer because it dawned on her for the first time that going home would never be the same. She saw the same things in her parents that Don did, but she didn't want to think about them. In a way, she didn't even want to talk about these things because if she did, they must be true. Both of her kids were in college and couldn't get away as often to visit their grandparents. It would be so hard for them to see Grandpa and Grandma this way. She squeezed Don's hand and then turned and stared out the window, wondering what they would discover on the next visit. It was something she didn't want to think about.

Something's Wrong Here

Right about now, your gut may be telling you something is amiss. Feelings of frustration, panic, and being overwhelmed accompany these thoughts, and before long, your head begins to spin with the thoughts of, *Where do I begin?* and *What if . . .?*

What you are experiencing is completely normal. You are in that group of people we call the Sandwich Generation. You still need to care for your children as they lean into their adult lives, but you need to care for your parents as well, even if they don't acknowledge it. It's a very difficult place, but you can make it easier on yourselves as well as your parents. In this book,

I will show you ways to deal with your parents' lifetime of accumulation in a simple, systematic approach, but you need to decide right now that you will actively manage this challenge rather than being passive and letting it manage you. The first thing you can do to avoid the flying brick is to be honest about the signs you are beginning to see in your parents.

At first, it's the little things. The once neatly manicured lawn isn't quite up to your dad's standards. The refrigerator is stuffed with leftovers and half-empty containers. Bills are overdue. You don't think much of it. After all, your parents are in their seventies or eighties. How many of your friends' parents still live in the family home? Besides, your mom and dad have earned the right to slow down a little. Who's keeping track of how neat the kitchen is anyway?

We see these signs and tend to ignore them for a lot of reasons. For one thing, we don't like to think about our parents growing old. We get stuck with this image of them, maybe right after retirement, when they're happy, full of life, and enjoying the freedom of not having to work. We also have an uncanny sense of knowing our place. For all our lives, our parents were the ones teaching us, nurturing us, helping us when we got in a jam, and telling *us* what to do. It just doesn't feel right to tell mom she needs to clean out her refrigerator more often.

We also ignore these early signs of our parents aging because they cause us to think the unthinkable: our parents can't live forever. This alone is a choking thought and surely one to bring tears to anyone's eyes.

I've worked with hundreds of baby boomers who come to me after a parent passes away, and the majority of them say things like, "I've been offering for years to help them deal with this stuff," or "We saw it coming, but we just couldn't bring ourselves to say or do anything." And now they are faced with what seems to be an impossible ordeal of deciding what to do with everything that's left behind. Believe me when I tell you that these family members are almost in a panic, and for good reason. If we let the inevitable sneak up on us, we will be totally unprepared for what needs to be done to handle our parents' estates. It's like being at the foot of a huge cliff we have to climb, but we have no ropes or climbing harness and no one to instruct us on how to get to the top.

The first thing you can do to prepare for the inevitable is to pay attention to the early signs of aging and illness. I'm not exaggerating when I say this is the *pivotal moment* in dealing with the scenario that has dropped on the laps of adult children. So many of my clients would have had a much easier time of it had they let those early signs begin a process that could have been so much more manageable than most people experience.

What are those early signs? Basically, any change you notice in your parents' behavior, attitudes, and surroundings can be an indicator. For example, suppose your dad always calls you on Sunday afternoon just to stay in touch. You come to expect those calls to the point you can almost set your watch by them. But lately, he's missed a couple of times. Or he called on Thursday instead of Sunday. Now, it may not be anything other than the fact he decided to call at a different time or just didn't feel like talking on Sunday. But it could be a sign that your dad is becoming a little confused, which is not uncommon in the aging process. No need to panic or intervene (unless there's some bizarre or distressing behavior that may require a professional assessment), but it's something you should note and a sign that should motivate you to keep paying closer attention.

Forgetfulness is one of the most common symptoms of the aging process, and by itself it is no real cause for concern. But there are other signs to notice:

- *Declining mobility.* Common ailments such as arthritis coupled with a loss of physical strength will make it hard for your parents to climb stairs, bend over and pick things up, perform household chores, and pursue hobbies they once were able to do.

- *Vision problems.* This is usually evidenced by difficulty in reading, sitting closer to the television than normal, a loss of peripheral vision or blurry vision, and squinting when they talk to you.

- *Loss of interest in favorite pastimes.* Your mom, who has sewn all her life, hasn't touched the sewing machine in months. Your dad seldom fusses in his garden anymore.

- *Irritability.* A once-gregarious and fun-loving parent rarely laughs and gets irritated and impatient easily.

- *Hearing loss.* You have to repeat yourself often or notice that the television volume is consistently loud. Your parent is often reluctant to admit there's a problem or to seek help.

- *Confusion.* Older people often misplace things or lose track of which day of the week it is.

- *Repetition.* Your parent tells the same story within a short time period.

- *Short-term memory loss.* Your mom forgets the boiling water on the stove. Your dad can't remember what day of the week it is.

- *Fatigue.* Your parent tires easily, needs to sit down and rest in the middle of an activity, nods off during the day, and sleeps more often and longer than usual.

- *Unopened mail.* It is not unusual for an older person who is struggling or having difficulty to let the mail pile up, often for weeks.

- *Changes in the home environment.* The house begins to look shabby. The yard becomes overgrown. The house has more clutter than usual. Simple maintenance tasks are left undone, such as cleaning the bathroom or emptying the trash, and there are strange odors in the home.

- *Unusual spending and/or hoarding (collecting).* You notice strange financial habits, especially ordering products from infomercials or an increase in the number of magazine subscriptions.

- *Preoccupation with finances.* Your mom expresses worries about money. Your dad complains more than usual about prices, taxes, and so on.

- *Change in appetite or not eating well.* Your parents appear to be losing weight or not eating well. Their kitchen cupboards are crammed with out-of-date canned goods or perhaps only boxes of cereal and crackers.

- *Staying alone, isolation.* Your parents used to enjoy visiting friends, but lately they make excuses and stay home alone, watching television or staring out the window.

- *Depression or anxiety.*

- *Bruising from stumbles or falls.*

Don't Panic, But Pay Attention

What should you do if you notice any of these signs of aging in your parents? Let's begin with what you *shouldn't* do, and that's overreact. The most common—and unhelpful—form of overreaction is to nag your parents about these things. That will only make the situation worse.

Most people react to these signs of aging by either forcing the issue with their parents or ignoring it. Don't try to fix it. Don't nag. Yet don't ignore these signs either. Just pay attention. Begin keeping a diary or log and write down what you notice. By paying attention and keeping a record, you will be able to objectively determine if these behaviors are happening infrequently and thus are not really troubling, or if they are getting worse and may need intervention.

The second thing you should do when you notice these signs is to begin to think about the future. This is one of the hardest things for boomers to do. No one likes to anticipate the inevitable. Deep down, we know no one lives forever and eventually our parents will pass on. But who likes to think about that? Yet I have found that when my clients allow themselves to think a few years ahead, they are much better prepared for the day when all they have left is their parents' empty house. It's the adult children who have been in denial who come really unglued when the end finally arrives. Being in denial will help no one, least of all your parents. Don't wait to deal with these issues until a moment of crisis, or that flying brick will turn into a boulder.

What to Notice About Your Parents' Aging Process

The following signs could mean that your parents need either to have someone to check on them daily or to move into assisted living:

- Declining mobility
- Vision problems
- Loss of interest in favorite pastimes
- Irritability

- Hearing loss
- Confusion
- Repetition
- Short-term memory loss
- Fatigue
- Unopened mail
- Changes in the home environment
- Unusual spending and/or hoarding (collecting)
- Preoccupation with finances
- Change in appetite or not eating well
- Staying alone, isolation
- Depression or anxiety
- Bruising from stumbles or falls

The Next Steps

As you begin to think about your parents' future, you will naturally and objectively begin thinking about what you might do as the next steps. For example, what will you do if one of your parents falls and is on bed rest for several weeks and the other parent is unable to care for her- or himself? What will you do if your parents refuse to move to assisted living but can't keep up with the demands of home ownership? What should you know about your parents' finances?

Again, this isn't the time to *do* anything but to simply make sure you aren't caught by surprise when it *is* time to do something. Thinking through the various scenarios that could happen to your parents will buy you a lot of peace of mind should anything serious happen in the future. And not to alarm you, but it will happen, and you don't ever want to face those things in a panic. When I work with adult children who have not adequately prepared for their parents' deaths, I often see that deer-in-the-headlights expression. They are literally immobilized by the task of going through their parents' estate. Allow these early signs of aging to prepare you mentally and emotionally for the journey ahead. Do your best to remain open and aware.

Another thing you can do when you begin to notice these early signs of infirmity in your parents is talk to your siblings. But if there ever is a minefield in dealing with the potential loss of our parents, it's in the landscape of family dynamics. Every family is different, and you know yours better than I do, but I can offer some general guidance you can put to use at this early stage: proceed gently and without overreacting. You may sense that your mom is beginning to slip, but your sister may see it entirely differently and resent your point of view. Ideally, you and your siblings will all be reading this book together and arrive at pretty much the same place when it comes to the early signs. Short of that, this is where keeping a record of these signs can be helpful in getting everyone in your family on the same page. It's one thing to say, "Dad's not himself anymore." It's a lot more convincing to open the pages of a notebook that shows dates and times when Dad ordered yet another subscription to *Popular Mechanics*.

If you are able to have this conversation with your siblings, remember, the goal is not to solve anything. It's too early for that and will only create more problems. The goal is for everyone to agree to one simple fact: "Dad is declining, so let's all pay attention and help him in any way we can." That's it. In my experience, hundreds of families would have saved themselves a lot of grief if at the outset they could have just agreed on these fairly recognizable signs. But it's extremely difficult to accept. Sometimes the heart is saying something, and the mind just doesn't want to hear it.

Once you're able to face and accept the natural aging process in your parents, you'll be better equipped to deal with what's coming next.

What Do I Do Now?

Current situation: anytime, but the earlier the better.

☑ *Begin a diary.* Record any unusual or alarming behavior that you notice in your parents.

☑ *Call or visit your parents.* From now on, pay specific attention to your parents' health and well-being. While you're at it, tell them you love them. There's no time like the present.

☑ *Begin a conversation with your siblings.* Gently and tactfully raise the issue of your parents' future.

Two

Planning for the Inevitable

As often happens, the phone call came to Diane in the middle of the night.

"Your father is here in our living room, and he's safe, but I think you need to come over and take him home."

Diane's heart sank. She had known something like this would happen. Her mom had passed away ten years ago, and over the past two years she noticed her dad becoming more confused and disoriented. Whenever she mentioned this to her brother, Bill, he just shrugged it off.

"You're overreacting, Sis," he countered when she mentioned yet another incident. "Dad's eighty-four years old! Of course he's going to forget some things, but it's a far cry from Alzheimer's. I think he's doing pretty well for his age."

And that's as far as those conversations went because Bill didn't want to face the situation. But Diane knew that things were getting worse, and she was worried that her dad's confusion and infirmity could result in an accident. She tried not to think about it, but it was a gnawing feeling she couldn't shake. Believe it or not, Dad still drove to the grocery store and did his best to prepare his own meals, occasionally going to the local diner where everyone knew him. But in recent visits, Diane was troubled by the mess in the kitchen, the molding food in the refrigerator, and an awful smell that suggested Dad was incontinent. And now this.

"We heard some noise in the kitchen, and when we got up to check it out, we saw your dad just standing there," her dad's neighbor explained when Diane arrived. Diane lived about twenty-five minutes away and was so grateful for a caring neighbor who was not upset by this middle-of-the-night intrusion. Her thoughts began to wander: *What if the neighbors had thought he was a burglar? He could have been accidentally shot!* Or what if her dad had walked to a busy street instead of to the neighbors' house? She didn't want to think about that either.

Apparently her dad wandered out into the winter night in only his pajamas—no shoes or socks—and somehow found his way into the neighbors' house. They got him to lie down on the couch, where he was now sleeping, wrapped in a blanket. Diane gently woke him, thanked the neighbors, and led her dad back into his home and sat by his bed until he fell back to sleep. He never said a word and didn't seem to know what was going on. Although Diane was exhausted, she couldn't sleep; so she sat in Dad's La-Z-Boy, trying to figure out what to do.

The next day, Diane called her brother and this time gave it to him straight. "Bill, this is serious. Dad wandered into the neighbor's house last night, and I'm worried that one of these days he'll walk into traffic. I'm here with him now, and he seems to be okay, but we've got to get him out of this house and into a place where he will have around-the-clock professional care." But Bill would hear none of it.

When Diane tried to talk her dad into moving, she was met with a stony glare. "I've lived here for longer than you've been alive, young lady, and I'm not about to move now! You'll have to carry me out on a stretcher!" Diane knew she was in for a huge challenge. She could just sense something horrible was going to happen to her dad, and this thought never allowed her any rest.

About a month after that incident, Diane and Bill's dad fell and was taken to the hospital with a concussion and a broken hip. It was his last home; within days he passed away. And then reality sank in. Diane and Bill were left with a house filled with sixty years of accumulation. They couldn't find any records to determine if it was paid for, which banks held their dad's accounts, whether or not he had left a will, or whether he had any debts that needed to be cleared.

That's right about the time people call me, usually in a crisis mode and wanting advice on how to deal with their parents' lifetime of accumulation. As I sorted through Diane and Bill's father's possessions, I thought how different it could have been if the family had prepared for something that all of us will have to face someday.

Boomer Denial

One of the things I've learned in my nearly twenty years of helping families settle the estates of their parents is how much we all avoid thinking about death. Intellectually, we know that if everything goes all right, we will be given our "threescore and ten,"[1] but emotionally we don't get too far beyond next month due to the rapid pace of our own lives. Even if we see an elderly parent on his deathbed, we hold out hope that he will recover, which may be admirable, but then becomes a form of denial that prevents us from facing and preparing for reality.

I've thought about this a lot, and while I can't prove it, I believe we baby boomers have a harder time dealing with the anticipation of our parents' passing than any previous generation. For one thing, our parents are living longer and generally are healthier going into their retirement years than their parents were. When you see mom and dad golfing together or traveling to exotic locations well into their seventies, you don't really think of them as old. It almost seems as if they will live forever. Most of our parents lost at least one of their parents at a fairly early age, which conditioned them to the realities of life. But we could be in our sixties and still watching our parents lead active lives.

It's also harder for boomers to think about the eventual passing of our parents because our culture is fixated on youthfulness, vitality, and an active lifestyle. Have you ever noticed how many advertisements feature maladies such as arthritis, high blood pressure, heart disease, and even incontinence? Instead of showing the reality of wrinkled and crippled older adults in wheelchairs, these ads feature smiling men and women with gray hair, playing with their grandkids, running marathons, or kayaking into the sunset.

It's a great way to sell a product, but it further insulates us from the truth we all have to face: even Lipitor won't keep your parents alive forever.

There's also the issue of having to switch roles, or parental role reversal. For all our lives, we've been going to our parents for help and advice. As we see our parents decline, we realize that now we are going to have to parent our parents, and that's an uncomfortable feeling.

But I think the primary reason so many of us avoid thinking about the inevitable is that once we accept the fact that our parents will someday be gone, we must also confront our own mortality. Logically, we're next in line. I don't know why Bill refused to move his father into assisted living, but I have a strong hunch: doing so would cause him to realize the same thing will eventually happen to him, and he just couldn't go there at the age of fifty-six.

Here's the bad news and the good news for all of us in the Sandwich Generation. The bad news is that, yes, we are next, and there will come a time when we may not be able to care for our homes or for ourselves. But the good news is that preparing for your parents' passing will also prepare *you* so that your kids never have to go through what you're going through right now. Your parents love you dearly and would never want you to experience the pain and distress of having to take care of their belongings on your own. Many parents just don't know how to get their affairs in order. As a loving parent, you can use what you learn in this book to make sure your children will be fully prepared as you age, which will give you peace of mind as you enter your own golden years.

Note to Parents

Telling your children you love them is a beautiful thing. Showing them you love them by handling your affairs while you are still able is a beautiful gift your children will never forget. Even if you are not here to see and hear their appreciation, take my word for it. If you don't know how to get your affairs in order, this book will help you. I encourage you to call professionals in your own community to find the right people to help you make these decisions now, before it is too late.

Can't We All Just Get Along?

The absolute best place to start the process of preparing for the inevitable is not with your parents but with your siblings. This is also the hardest place to start. But if you and your siblings are all in agreement about these issues, the rest of the process will be relatively easy. Trust me on this: the most serious problems in estate liquidation come from surviving children who can't get along. They have avoided the difficult conversations and decisions until they are hit with them in the sudden crisis of infirmity and/or death of a parent, and it goes downhill from there. The human brain just isn't capable of handling such an emotional load. On the other hand, I've had rare instances where it was clear that family members had been talking to one another, and even if they didn't agree on everything, they had established open and honest communication that allowed them to sort out their differences. Here's how you can join the latter group.

You can start the process by contacting your siblings and inviting them to meet you at a restaurant or coffee shop. If you meet in a public place, you will be less likely to let your emotions take over. And most of the sibling problems in my business come from a sister-in-law or brother-in-law—your wife innocently speaks up for the dining room set, you feel you have to defend her, and then the fighting begins. This is why I recommend keeping this meeting just between siblings.

The goal of this meeting is to get the issues on the table and let everyone say what's on their minds. The invitation could go like this: "Mom and Dad are in pretty good health, but they are having some troubles. What do we do if they become infirm or die suddenly? Let's go around the table and see what we're all thinking." And then set these ground rules:

1. Everyone has a chance to speak before any questions or comments from anyone else.
2. No decisions will be made; it's just a sibling meeting to gather everyone's thoughts.

3. Everyone will read *The Boomer Burden*.

4. All siblings will meet in a few months to continue the conversation (try to set a date before everyone leaves, if possible).

5. Agree that if anything should happen to your parents in the interim, all siblings will be in constant contact with one another.

A conversation like this is beneficial because it will help you and your siblings see one another's perspectives and unique points of view. For example, if your children are grown, you will be more likely to want to take an active role in your parents' situation than a sibling who still has children in the house. In a scenario like that, it often defuses any potential guilt or resentment if you say something like, "Lisa, I know you're right in the thick of things with your kids still home while mine are all out on their own, and I have more time. So don't feel bad if I'm able to help Mom and Dad more right now." The more you and your siblings can approach this process as a team, communicating regularly and doing things out in the open, the better things will be when a crisis hits.

I encourage teamwork among siblings because, with most families, these situations have a tendency to fall on one sibling more than the others. This can stir resentment, and there is no room for that in the midst of a crisis. When you and your siblings do not work as a team, it adds greater challenge at a time when focus and working together is needed more than ever.

Note to Parents

Wouldn't it be nice if your children didn't have to go to these lengths? If you sit down with your children and discuss your wishes, hand all of your legal documents to them, and leave clear instructions, they won't have to guess or bicker about what to do.

Having *That Conversation* with Your Parents

If one or both of your parents are still living and mentally competent, the next step in helping them (and your family) prepare for the inevitable is to begin talking to your parents about the future. But I have to warn you—you might not get very far at first. Your parents are part of a generation that lived through the Depression, a world war, and you! They tend to be tight-lipped about personal things and will, at first, brush you off, either politely or abruptly. So how you approach the subject is important.

For example, it is absolutely imperative that your parents have an updated will, but don't expect them to talk about this with you if you visit them in the hospital and one of the first things you say is, "Have you made out your will yet?" How would you feel if your kids did that to you in a similar situation? Instead, try to find a time when your parents are in their own home and you are enjoying a normal conversation. One of the best ways to bring up the subject is to focus more on yourself than on your parents. You could say, for example, "I read the other day in the news about how many people in my age group have not made out wills, so Marci and I went right out and had one drawn up. I couldn't believe how easy it was, and it sure feels great knowing that the government isn't going to decide what happens to our stuff. How about you guys?"

Conversation Starters for You and Your Parents

It is never easy to talk with your parents about future issues. Here are some conversation starters that will make it more comfortable for you and your parents:

- "Mom, you've been such a great help to me over the years. I don't know what I'd ever do without you."
- "Mom and Dad, sometimes I worry about you living all alone. Are there any things we could do to help you?"
- "Dad, when Uncle Jim passed away, his family fought for weeks over things. Do you ever worry that Mike and I will be like that?"

- "Ever since Mom's stroke, I've been worried about your meals and things. Are you doing all right?"

- "Jim and I started looking closer at our retirement account, and we'd love to pick your brain about all the things we need to know about retirement."

- "Dad, do you ever worry about Mom if she had to go it alone without you?"

Parents, listen to your children. And children, listen to your parents. This is a critical conversation for all of you, and you want to make sure you communicate well. Just like when we were kids in school, don't be afraid to raise your hand and ask questions. Making assumptions or guessing about what the other one wants can be dangerous and lead to places you don't want to go. Remember what your teachers used to tell you: there's no such thing as a dumb question.

By making these questions conversational rather than confrontational, you stand a much better chance of engaging your parents and minimizing their natural tendency to avoid the subject. The immediate goal here is not to get your parents to make out a will, but to begin a conversation and create an environment of trust that you will need for further conversations. Again, put yourself in your father's shoes. He's usually been the one to give advice and offer guidance on things like finances, mortgages, important decisions, and so on. It's tough, especially for older men, to accept this kind of help from anyone much younger than they are, let alone their own child. Pressuring your parents on issues such as their will or the status of their finances will surely raise their defenses. Instead of telling them what to do, show them what you are doing and let them discover the need to do it themselves.

Once you have the initial conversation and sense that your parents are comfortable talking about the what-ifs, try to avoid discussing these types of things every time you're together. They will need time to think about and process each conversation and may become resistant if every time you visit, you bring up something about their future. If your parents don't feel pressured, they may even initiate a conversation without your prodding. Sometimes though, gentle nudging is necessary.

Assuming you had that first conversation with your parents, it went well, and you feel that your parents are willing to continue talking, here are some topics you eventually will need to cover with them:

Assigning an executor and power of attorney. At some point, your parents need to give someone the power to execute their wishes if they are unable to make their own decisions. Usually this will be a family member, and often it is the oldest child. But here's where things can get dicey because parents usually don't like to make decisions that could be viewed to favor one child over another. I have known parents who chose to make their children coexecutors of their estate, but this can be a very tricky situation, especially if there is a difference of opinion among the siblings. Naming one person as executor (or executrix) might be more prudent unless you have your reasons otherwise.

Location of important papers. You or a sibling needs to know the location of your parents' bank records, insurance policies, investment accounts, loans and mortgages, pension information, deeds and titles, and so on. At this point, you do not need to see the contents of any of these documents—you just need to know where they are kept. If they are kept in a safe or strong box, make sure you know the combination or have access to a key.

Monthly bills and expenses. Ask your parents to show you their system for paying their monthly bills: utilities, telephone, car payments, credit cards, and so on. I've found that as people get older, they are likely to either forget or ignore these bills, so you may need to check with your parents regularly to make sure they are paying them. I know of some cases where one of the adult children comes in once a month to help parents handle these monthly expenses. If your last surviving parent dies suddenly, you will need to close out these accounts, so make sure you know where they keep their bills.

Prescription and other health-related information. What medications do your parents take regularly? Are the prescriptions up-to-date? Would you know where to find their medicines? Imagine your parents being totally dependent on you for medication, and make sure you know what to do if that happens.

Division of assets. You want to make sure your parents have a will. It's really their business as to what they want done with their assets, but you can help them understand the options that are available to them. If possible, arrange for them to talk with a certified financial planner or estate planning attorney who can explain issues related to estate taxes.

End-of-life decisions. This is one of the most difficult areas for any of us to consider, but at some point your parents need to decide to what extent they want medical personnel to extend their lives.

Funeral plans. Funeral arrangements are not something pleasant for most people to talk about, yet it will give your parents peace of mind to know that all the arrangements are discussed ahead of time.

Note to Parents

All of these are vital subjects that you should be discussing with your children or heirs. If you should be rendered unconscious, in a vegetative state, or pass away suddenly, a true emergency is in the making and everyone will feel disconnected for a while. If your children are equipped with your decisions about these issues, you are empowering them during an overwhelming time.

Home Sweet Home

One of the most difficult areas of preparation has to do with the family home. As your parents get older, they will find it harder and harder to maintain a large home. But they generally won't admit it and will resist any suggestion to move into either a smaller home or apartment or any kind of assisted-care arrangement. Here's why.

It is their home—a warm and comfortable nest loaded with pleasant memories. In many ways, your parents' identity revolves around their home. It may be where you took your first steps, opened hundreds of Christmas presents, and shared thousands of meals. It's where Grandma baked cookies and Grandpa tended a garden. So much of what's important to your parents' lives—and yours—is in that house. And they worked hard to pay for it, which is another reason they don't want to move: they fear the high cost of assisted living and worry that all they have saved, along with the equity from their house, will be eaten up in monthly rent. Finally, the prospect of selling their place and moving is overwhelming. They know they've accumulated a lifetime of stuff, and they just don't have the energy or motivation to figure out what to do with it all.

However, many senior adults have another fear: getting rid of their belongings reminds them of their own mortality.

Because this conversation is so difficult, most people put it off until it's too late. John and Elizabeth were in their mideighties and were doing pretty well despite the fact that they lived in a two-story home on a half-acre lot. Sarah, their fifty-seven-year-old daughter, had begun to notice some basic maintenance tasks were being ignored, such as laundry stacking up for several weeks because the laundry room was in the basement, flower beds sporting more weeds than perennials, and food rotting in the refrigerator. Both John and Elizabeth had lost a good deal of weight, leading Sarah to believe they weren't eating well. She gently suggested they might enjoy living with other people their age in a nice retirement community just a few blocks from their home, but her parents put up such a fuss about it she never mentioned it again.

Then Elizabeth fell down the basement stairs on her way to the laundry room and had to be hospitalized for several weeks. John was nearly helpless without his beloved wife by his side and was soon in the hospital himself after suffering a stroke. It was obvious that they would never be able to live in their house, but now the family had to make some hard decisions . . . and with lightning speed.

Before we explore options for providing a safe environment for a parent in poor health, I need to confess that I'm not an expert in this subject, even though I work with a lot of older people. But I have worked closely with a geriatric care manager, Jennifer Szakaly, who has given me and countless clients a wealth of information on the subject of caring for our older parents. One thing she emphasizes is that you always have more options than you think *if* you plan ahead. According to Jennifer, most people wait too long to act and then find themselves having to react in a panic. She recommends a gradual transition rather than trying to move your parents directly from their home into an assisted-care arrangement. For example, most retirement communities offer respite care so that a parent could go into a safer environment for anywhere from twenty-four hours to thirty days. Often this provides enough relief and proper treatment, allowing the parent to move back into his home. It also is less traumatic for the parents since they will still have their home. They also have the option of twenty-four-hour care in their own home if it is financially feasible, or a widowed parent might even consider a roommate.

I have found that people are more successful in encouraging their parents of the need to eventually move into a safer living arrangement if they talk with their parents about it while the parents are younger, healthy, and active as opposed to waiting until a real crisis—physical and mental—sets in. (In chapter 4, I will go into greater detail about how to handle a residential change when the time is right.) Encourage your parents to visit a progressive, well-managed senior community where they can see other older adults enjoying themselves in a social environment. Many of the new retirement communities are built around activities such as golf, tennis, hiking, and gardening. When you mention assisted living to your parents, they most likely recall the old nursing homes where elderly parents were sent, basically, to die in small cubicles with little more than a bed and a television set. According to Jennifer, one of the most common fears of seniors is being left alone. Seeing people their own age in an active, cheerful environment often takes away a lot of their fears about moving. Many of these communities will provide a trial weekend to let your parents experience today's assisted-living environment.

The key is to present their new living arrangement in the most positive way possible. Try not to focus on the downside of your parents staying in their home—they won't see it that way. Instead, cast a vision of how much better their lives can be in a new setting surrounded by new friends with whom they can share their interests.

Having said all that, your parents may dig their heels in and refuse to move. If that happens, here are some things you should do for their protection and for your own peace of mind:

Consult with a geriatric care manager. This person can be a vital resource for the whole family.

Utilize community resources. Meals on Wheels or similar programs will help ensure your parents' nutritional needs are met and may avoid potentially dangerous kitchen accidents. Schools and churches or synagogues also offer volunteer resources, including someone stopping by regularly to chat and make sure everything is okay. Check with the senior citizens center in their community for a list of resources for your parents.

Consider hiring a home health care nurse. For a nominal fee that may be covered by your parents' insurance or Medicare, a nurse will visit your parents on a weekly basis to check their blood pressure, monitor their medication, and observe their overall health.

Make frequent visits and daily telephone calls. Enlist the help of your siblings and set up a schedule for regular visits and phone calls, checking with one another to compare notes.

Alert your parents' neighbors. Make an effort to contact one or two neighbors with whom you feel comfortable and let them know of your concerns. Ask them to keep the conversation private. Innocent or idle gossip could potentially set up another "crime scene" of people who are eager to get their hands on your parents' valuables. Give the neighbors your phone number, and ask them to call you if they notice anything out of the ordinary (like finding your dad in their house at 3 a.m. in his pajamas).

Notify local law enforcement and emergency personnel. Be specific about your parents' physical and mental conditions so if they were called to respond to an emergency, they would be prepared.

Install a home alarm or video monitoring system. Most security companies provide these services at a reasonable cost.

Consider ordering a medical alert device. You can order electronic sensors that when worn on a necklace will activate an emergency center if the wearer falls.

No one likes to think about these inevitable issues with their parents, let alone prepare for them. But like most things in life, planning ahead will make future events easier to handle. In the next chapter, we will continue your preparation by discussing the most important documents to keep your parents' estate from becoming a battle zone: the will and the durable power of attorney.

What Do I Do Now?

Current situation: you begin to notice your parents failing.

☑ *Meet with your siblings.* If possible, arrange a face-to-face meeting and let all siblings give their perspectives on your parents' health and future.

☑ *Recruit your parents' neighbors.* Give your phone number to at least two of your parents' neighbors, and remember to get theirs too.

☑ *Schedule the conversation.* Set a deadline for when you will attempt to talk with your parents about their future.

Three

Where's the Will?

Carolyn was ninety-six years old and had a lovely three-bedroom home filled with antiques passed down from previous generations. It was obvious that Carolyn and her predecessors had taken great pride in these heirlooms because they were in immaculate condition. She had done everything right: she left all items in their original condition, she knew the history and stories that went with each piece, and she kept them out of direct sunlight and away from the heat vents.

I met Carolyn six months prior to her passing. Her two children were present, and everyone wanted to know the values of Carolyn's possessions from her mother's and grandmother's estates dating back to the 1850s. Earlier, the children spoke with me privately and told me their mother had not prepared a will and asked me to try to impress upon her the importance of doing so. As I examined each piece, I spoke with Carolyn about the importance of making out a will so she could determine what would happen to all of these valuable antiques, but Carolyn was adamant. "I don't need a will. I've written on a piece of notebook paper my wishes for my children, and that's good enough. If it isn't, then they can just fight over it." And so they would. The children looked at me and grimaced. They knew the complications that awaited them if their mother didn't draft a legal will: potential years of red tape with hefty attorney fees.

Carolyn eventually passed away peacefully, but there was little peace for the family. No one ever found the handwritten note, so it became a game of

"Mom said I could have this," and "No, she promised that to me." Sadly, it was years before the estate was settled, and no one was happy with the outcome.

I wish this story was an exception, but in my experience, it is the norm. According to a Harris Interactive survey, 55 percent of Americans have not bothered to see an attorney to prepare a will.[1] That means if your neighbor has drafted a will, you probably haven't. Have you? It also means there's a good chance your parents have not formally designated what is to happen to their possessions by executing a will.

You Die Only Once, So Why Not Do It Right?

I'm not sure why so many of us have not followed through on the simple process of completing a will, but I'm guessing it's part procrastination and part avoidance of thinking about death. Unlike Carolyn, most of us agree that we need a will, and we all plan to get around to it someday. But when you are in your forties or fifties, you just don't spend much time thinking about your eventual passing. Because you are in good health and believe you have at least another thirty years or so of life ahead of you, you don't feel any urgency to take care of these details. Yet one of the worst things you can do to your family is to leave them guessing about who is going to get your possessions after you die, as many of my clients will attest. Long after my work is done for them in assessing the value of their parents' estate, they are locked in battle with one another and the courts. It is costly, both financially and emotionally, and unnecessary.

One of the reasons people sometimes procrastinate is that they think a will is a complicated legal document that requires a difficult process. If a person has not made out a will by the age of seventy, it seems even more daunting. But in reality, making out a will is a fairly simple process that doesn't have to be any more complicated or time-consuming than going out to lunch with a friend. Some basic information, then, will help you understand why it's important that your parents create a will.

A will not only determines what is to be done with the deceased person's property but also does two other very important things: it names a guardian or executor, and it promotes family harmony, a loving and lasting gift. It is also strongly recommended that the executor named by your parents be given durable power of attorney. This, too, is a relatively simple process that enables the executor to make decisions and transfer your parents' assets as needed.

A last will and testament is a legal document that gives clear instructions about what to do with your property after your death and how death taxes, if any, are to be paid, along with final expenses that would include any debt and administrative costs. It states who is to receive the property and in what amounts. A will may also be used to name a guardian for any minor children or to create a trust to handle an estate inheritance to protect spendthrift children or others. Finally, and this is important in the case of your parents, a will can be used to name a personal representative or executor to handle property and affairs from the time of death until an estate is settled.

Sometimes people will avoid making out a will because they don't think they have all that much to leave behind. "We're not too worried about Mom not having a will because all she has are some knickknacks and furniture" is a sentiment I often hear. But even if the few items do not have significant monetary value, those candlesticks and teacups have sentimental value. (More on the difference between monetary and sentimental value in chapter 9.) Regardless of the size of the estate or potential value of the possessions, everyone should have a will!

Each state has its own requirements for creating a will, but three factors are fairly universal:

1. The will must be written, dated, and signed.

2. The person who makes the will (called a *testator*) must be legally competent, acting voluntarily, and at least eighteen years old.

3. The signing of the will must be witnessed by at least two legally competent individuals. Witnesses do not need to know the contents of the will and should not be beneficiaries (persons who would receive something) of the will. They should also be disinterested parties. (A number of states require that a notary public be a signatory to a will.)

You do not have to hire an attorney to make out a will, though I highly recommend it. The law is multifaceted, and all kinds of scenarios can erupt. Wouldn't you want the best legal representation possible if something went wrong? Depending on the complexity of the will, it will initially cost a few hundred dollars to have an attorney explain your options (especially death tax issues that could negatively affect the overall distribution of the property) and then draw up the document. But what Carolyn wrote on notebook paper in her own handwriting could have served as a legal will if it were witnessed and notarized (although the validity of a homemade will would be up to the discretion of the courts or state law, who will want to make sure it is sound and interpretable). Making out a will can be fairly easy if you have competent guidance along the way.

You can change or update a will at any time, and it is a good idea to review your will as your circumstances change. An amendment to the will is referred to as a *codicil*. Again, I recommend you consult an attorney when you change a will as some changes are minor, and some are considered major. Here are some reasons for updating a will:

- The family changes due to a birth, adoption, marriage, divorce, or death (in a divorce, a will automatically excludes the former spouse unless it expressly states otherwise).
- Major changes occur in the amount of property owned.
- Tax laws change (federal and state).
- Residence changes from one state to another.
- The executor or guardian can no longer serve.
- You decide—for any reason—to change the distribution of your property.

Remember, along with drawing up a will, you must be extra careful to match the beneficiaries in your will to your other financial assets as well. Anything that has to do with money (investments, bank accounts, mutual funds, life insurance policies, retirement accounts, and so on) requires you to assign a beneficiary. If, for example, decades ago you listed an ex-spouse or someone you are no longer involved with as a beneficiary on your life insurance policy, the policy may not go to the loved one you've currently named in your will but rather to the person listed on that policy. This is an important issue that should be discussed with an attorney to make sure all your wishes are fulfilled.

That's about it, except for two important details—keeping the will in a safe place and making sure the family knows where it is kept. The signed original document should be stored in a fireproof lock box, bank safe-deposit box, or some other place where it will be permanently protected. And the executor should know where the key is or have a key in his or her possession. A copy of the will that notes the location of the original document should be given to the executor or the loved one's attorney. I also recommend that all members of the immediate family be given the location of the will, just as a precaution.

A Willful Checklist

- Determine if your parents have made out a will.
- Know the location and the executor of the will.
- If your parents have not made out a will, explain the value of having one.
- Show them a sample form for a will or living trust.
- Give them a list of estate planning attorneys in their city.

If There Is No Will

If your parents are living and have not made out a will, you should explain to them what will happen if they pass away without a will (in legal terms, this is called being *intestate*). Many older people assume that their children will work things out between themselves, and even if there are disagreements along the way, everything will eventually be fine. Unfortunately, when a person dies without a will, the state has the legal responsibility to handle the affairs of the deceased.

When there is no valid will, a probate court appoints an administrator to handle the decedent's affairs, and his or her property is distributed according to a formula fixed by that state's laws. There is no wiggle room in these laws, regardless of what proof you may have that Mom or Dad intended to leave the house to you. After the taxes, funeral expenses, and administrative costs are paid, the remaining property is divided among the surviving family members, but not necessarily as the parent wanted. The laws in each state are very specific as to how the property is distributed when there is no will, including which relatives have priority. In other words, when someone dies without a will, the state mandates a default plan and determines who gets what.

What Is Probate?

Without going into all the legal details, *probate* is the process of determining how to distribute property from the estate of the person who has died to his or her beneficiaries. The term *probate* refers to "proving" the existence of a valid will or, if there is no will, "proving" who the proper legal heirs are. This process can take anywhere from six months to two years, depending on tax issues, debt, and state requirements. The laws of probate vary among states; therefore, you should seek legal counsel in the state where your parents resided.

Here's what really happens. Let's say your dad died several years ago, and your mom just passed away recently. At some point after the funeral, you and your siblings begin looking for the will and soon discover none exists. You're not too concerned because you and your siblings are extremely close and have no intention of fighting over your mother's property. You decide to begin by going through the house to take what you want to keep and then sell the rest and divide up the money from the sale. At that point, you might be guilty of planning larceny because none of those things belongs to you. They are owned by the estate of your deceased parent, and you do not have a legal right to them until the state determines how they should be distributed. The same is true for the house.

This scenario assumes a family that is close-knit and intends to divide everything equally and generously. Imagine what can happen if there are rivalries or difficult relationships in your family.

If your last surviving parent died without drawing up a will, don't panic. Your parent's property and possessions will ultimately be divided between you and your siblings though it could take longer than you would like, and you may not agree with the court's distributions. You can minimize the amount of time it takes and thus the legal costs involved by not contesting anything. The court will most likely rule that the house is to be sold and the money divided among the surviving children. As for the possessions in the house, the court may allow you and your siblings to try to divide the contents yourselves, and my advice is to do your best to keep this from turning into a fight; the court will step in if a fight ensues, and that will involve more legal costs.

Key lesson here: make sure your parents draw up a will, and make sure you know where it is.

An Alternative to a Will

Before we leave the subject of wills, I'd like to explain how a living revocable trust works and how it might be a better alternative to a will. Basically, a living trust is very similar to a will, except that the settling of the estate will go much faster because it does not need to be administered by the probate court.

To create a living trust, you create a legal document called a *declaration of trust* or *living revocable trust*. In some ways it is similar to a will in that it gives instructions for the distribution of your property after you die. In addition, you will avoid what is termed a *living probate* or *guardianship* should you become unable to handle your personal and financial affairs during your lifetime. With a living trust, you typically name yourself as the trustee or person in charge of the trust property, transfer ownership of your property to the trustee, and then name the people or organizations you want to inherit the property after your death, your beneficiaries. You also will be asked to name a "successor trustee" who will carry out your wishes as described in the trust.

As with a will, in a living trust you can change these designations anytime you want, and you can also revoke the trust anytime. When you die, the successor trustee transfers ownership of the property in the trust to those people or organizations you designated. The process can be completed in a few weeks, which is faster than the normal time it takes a will to be admitted to probate. So the primary advantages of a living will are simplicity, privacy, and quicker time span.

I recommend discussing both options with an estate planning attorney. In fact, if it were my parents, I would insist they use an attorney for executing a will or living trust, even if I had to pay the fees myself, which brings me to my final word on wills and trusts.

Remember, if your parents have not made out a will, they may be fearful that it is a complicated and costly process, or they are reluctant to think about their eventual passing.

Note to Parents

Passing away without a will is a big no-no. It is not a matter of if, but *when* our time comes.

I have given you enough information to help you convince them that making out a will is relatively simple. Regarding their reluctance to talk about their own passing, you know your parents better than I do, but I recommend gentle persistence. Don't nag or bring up the subject every time you see your parents. But do tell them the story of Carolyn. Remind them what could happen if they die without a will. Most men of this generation are reluctant to have the government get anything, so appeal to your dad's independent spirit and show him how a will can keep the government from getting more than it is rightly entitled to. Avoid campaigning for specific items as that will only create more resistance because your parents don't want to feel forced into choosing sides.

Make this an important task on your to-do list because if your parents have a will when they die, they will have given you and your siblings a gift far greater than the value of all of their possessions.

What Do I Do Now?

Current situation: your parents do not have their will and other affairs in order.

☑ *Go online, and Google "will."* Use a search engine to look up the word *will* on the Internet, and read at least three entries explaining wills.

☑ *Make sure you have a will or revocable trust.* If you don't, schedule an appointment with an estate planning attorney—the sooner, the better.

☑ *Be a good example.* Give your parents a copy of your will, and ask them if they have one.

Four

When Reality Sinks In

I do a lot of public speaking, and as you might expect, many people come up to me after the event to ask advice on their parents' estates. Sometimes their questions are of a personal nature, and they want to consult with me in private. That's how I met Steve.

A really sharp guy in his midfifties, Steve had driven quite a distance to hear me speak, so I knew something was weighing on his mind. I learned that he and his wife, Debbie, had recently moved from the West Coast to be closer to Debbie's ailing parents. Debbie's dad had been hospitalized for the third time in a year for heart problems, and her mom suffered a variety of physical ailments. Her parents had lived in the same house for more than forty years, and though both Steve and Debbie knew something had to be done, they were at a loss as to what to do.

"My wife and I have been telling her folks for years that they need to move into a retirement community because their house is a real mess," Steve told me over a cup of coffee. "You can hardly walk through the place without tripping over piles of stuff they just can't seem to get rid of: fifty years of *National Geographic*. Newspapers and mail-order catalogs dating back two decades are stacked around the perimeter of the dining room. Open one of Mom's kitchen cupboards, and dozens of Cool Whip containers fall out. And the basement is literally floor-to-ceiling with just about anything you can imagine, and what won't fit there has overflowed into the garage, so they can't even put their car in it. But what really scares us is their physical and mental state. They never go out. Mom has fallen a couple of times, and the only food in the place is cereal or vanilla pudding. No milk. No meat. Just half-empty boxes of cereal in several cupboards and stacks of dirty cereal bowls in the sink."

Steve went on to tell me that Debbie had tried for many years to get her parents to move to an assisted-living facility nearby that provides various living arrangements from independent living condos all the way up to critical care. "It would be perfect for them, and they have many friends living there, but we just can't get them to even consider it," Steve said with more than a little exasperation. "Is there any way you can help us? This situation has even taken a toll on our marriage."

I agreed to meet with Debbie, and I found her to be a deeply hurting woman. She looked stunned and overwhelmed. That flying brick must have really hit her hard. One minute she would be in tears, and the next minute she would be lashing out in anger—a kind lady who clearly had been affected by the difficult decisions ahead of her. I learned that she and Steve had three children—one a freshman in high school, a son in elementary school, and a daughter who would be getting married in a month. Talk about being right in the thick of things!

"I feel horrible that I'm so angry over this, but at this time in my life, I just can't handle it," Debbie sobbed. "I've talked to Mom until I am blue in the face about cleaning up, and she has had decades to do it a little bit at a time. We've offered to help her, or she could have gotten some help from the kids in the neighborhood. It's almost like she is intentionally leaving this burden for us to clean up, and it is weighing very heavily on us. In a way, she is making me feel like it is *our* responsibility to clean up her mess. Right now, I am feeling angry, and then I feel guilty because I feel angry! I'm not sure what to feel other than completely overwhelmed. Is this normal?"

Yes, it is.

I've met with so many Debbies before. It breaks my heart to see good people who have done all the right things and are diligently caring for their families when it hits them: *Mom and Dad need my help. They aren't going to live forever, and I don't know what to do. I think my life is getting ready to really shift, and it worries me because I don't know what to expect.*

If it's any consolation, millions of families this year will be right where Debbie was: literally caught between raising their own families and having to care for parents who might be uncooperative. It's not a fun place to be, so in this chapter I will help you avoid the immobilization that comes from the panic and offer strategies for resolving the tough issues you will have to face.

Clearing Out Some of the Mess

I have found enough bread twister ties, paper clips, rubber bands, girdle hooks, bobby pins, pencil nubs, plastic bags, and Cool Whip containers to go around the equator at least twice in my career. That is not an exaggeration.

In chapter 11, I will go into the basics of dealing with all the contents of your parents' home, but at this part of the process, when one or both of your parents are still living in the house, you may need to do something about the clutter if it is overwhelming. For one thing, it's a safety hazard. Piles of stuff throughout the house are opportunities for your parents to trip and become injured. (For the record, I have even tripped and fallen under some of these conditions.) And too many stacks of newspapers or cardboard boxes present a fire hazard. Besides, a little work now will make things easier later.

I recommend the direct approach whenever possible. Share with your parents that you want to help them get rid of some of the clutter in their home. It might work, but probably won't. Your mom thinks it makes absolute sense to keep old bread bags in a drawer, and your dad will not want to part with his stacks of *Outdoor Life,* so if you feel they are not approachable about this, leave it be. But since I believe in being direct, I highly suggest open communication with your mom and dad at all times. "Mom, I'm a little concerned, and I am hoping you can put my mind at ease. All those catalogs and magazines stacked up are going to trip you one day, and I don't ever want that to happen. Please let me take some things out of your way." Then put them in the trunk of your car and take them to where they really belong: a recycle bin.

Each time you visit your parents, try to remove at least one bag or box of these types of items and put them into your car. It will make their environment safer and make you feel better too.

Many parents keep things dating back to when their kids still lived at home. I've seen homes where 1960s-era clothing hung in empty bedrooms. You may run across your old clothes, schoolbooks, athletic equipment, trophies, report cards, and the like. The best way to get those things out of the house is to tell your parents you'd really like to remove them to give them some extra space and that the time has long passed since it was your responsibility to do so. What you do with these items is up to you. You could find a good charity or donate them to an organization such as a school theater that can use them for props. Encourage your siblings to do the same thing with their own items. You might be surprised at how much fun your kids will have seeing all of your old clothes and stuff. This pains me to say, but most of our childhood toys are now considered vintage and, therefore, somewhat collectible. My daughter is still fascinated by the fact that her mom grew up watching black-and-white TV and had only one rotary telephone in the whole house.

For now, don't attempt to remove anything that might have sentimental or monetary value such as coins, collections, figurines, silver, framed art, antiques, or estate jewelry. These need to remain with your mom and dad until they want to pass them on to family members.

If your parents distribute some of the heirlooms prior to death, the fighting will be minimized, and everyone will know your mom and dad made their decisions. An added bonus is that your parents can see the joy on the recipients' faces when given the item. Sadly, many parents do not want to do that because they feel they might hurt someone's feelings. It is still the parents' responsibility to communicate with the children what items they would like to give to each child. If they do not, encourage your parents to create a master list. (Discourage the use of stickers on the bottom of each item. Stickers fall off, fade, and can be switched or removed by unscrupulous children or heirs.)

A master list is a documented inventory of all the heirlooms your parents want to pass down. It can be handwritten or, if created on a computer, printed and signed. Each item is listed with the child's name to whom they want to give it: Sam gets Grandfather's desk, Becky gets the silver flatware, David gets Dad's guns, and so on. Then make sure each child gets a signed, identical copy of this list. If these instructions are in Mom or Dad's actual handwriting, children rarely contest. They might get their noses out of joint, but they will, at some point, get over it.

Besides, in fairness to other siblings or family members, you shouldn't take it upon yourself to either lay claim to valuables or remove them to sell. The goal here is to minimize the clutter for your parents' safety and prepare for a much easier transition when the time comes to completely empty the house.

The Paperaholic

You may think I'm exaggerating when it comes to the volume of stuff I find when I'm called to help liquidate an estate, but if you haven't been to your parents' home in a while, you may be in for a shock. I recall the time I was asked to clear out a 1920s-era house. The executor gave me the key to the front door, but when I turned the key and tried to push open the door, I couldn't move it. I went around to the side door, the back door—same problem. Finally my assistant and I put our shoulders to the door and slowly pushed it open enough to squeeze ourselves inside. We discovered the doors wouldn't open because there were stacks of paper and other debris all over the place, right up to the doors and covering every inch of the house.

The paper and debris were up to our knees on the first floor and on the second floor, up to our chests. We discovered stacks of mail that hadn't been opened since 1964. Among other things, we found several loaded guns, unopened bills, financial documents, newspapers, magazines, and countless personal items. It took us nine days and four commercial-sized Dumpsters (that weighed thirty-nine thousand pounds) to clear everything out! The homeowner had died several years prior, but when the family members visited the house after his death, they just gave up and let it sit until the city stepped in and demanded the property be cleaned up. It was, after all, a fire hazard and would surely go up in smoke if anyone got near it with a match. This, of course, is an extreme example, but it can get this way if left unattended. It is more common than you think.

Please, don't let that happen to you or someone you know. If your parents are still alive, do whatever you can to get rid of clutter that has no value. It will be exceptionally difficult for you to push aside your own feelings and bewilderment. All of your questions as to "why did Mom and Dad do this to us?" will probably never be answered in their entirety, forming a line of questioning that will only drive you crazy if you follow it to seek the answers. Be kind to yourself. Do your best to be understanding, and if you can't be understanding, that's okay too. Let compassion override anger, and do your best to forgive. Life will resume for you after all of this is ironed out; I promise.

Is It Time for Mom and Dad to Move?

One of the most paralyzing realities you will have to deal with is the awareness that your parents cannot care for themselves. At some point, you will know the time has come for a change in their living situation. This is usually precipitated by a crisis event such as a fall, accident in the kitchen, or wandering and not finding the way back home.

Many people panic when this happens to their parents, and they rush to decisions that are not always helpful. You really need to step back a bit, collect your thoughts, and try to objectively assess your situation. What exactly is the status of your parents' health? What are their living conditions like? Are they eating right? Are they keeping up with their regular monthly bills, such as utilities and phone? Are their driver's licenses current, and should they be driving? Are there safety issues, such as being too infirm to climb stairs or cook? Will they talk with you about their situation? Do they have support from neighbors, a church, or senior citizens center? If you have siblings, are they aware of your parents' situation?

When we discover that our parents are entering a phase of their lives that clearly signals they may not be with us much longer, we generally respond emotionally, which is understandable. This is why it is so important for you to gain as much factual information as possible so that your intellect will begin to bypass some of your emotions. There is absolutely nothing wrong with tears and emotions, but positive results come from clear thinking. There will come a time when tears will no longer help your beloved parent, but a stable, clear-thinking approach will be a great asset to everyone.

Gaining specific information about your parents' health is a tremendous challenge. More than likely, your parents will downplay their physical conditions, though sometimes they will actually exaggerate it. What you need is an accurate appraisal of your parents' mental and physical health. Since a physician cannot give you any information on your parents' health issues due to confidentiality laws,[1] try accompanying your parents when they have a doctor's appointment, and talk with the doctor about your concerns. The doctor may be able to either put your mind at ease or help you understand how you may be able to monitor your parents' health. It might be advisable to make sure your parents have selected someone or offered to assign power of attorney to a trusted individual in the event they become incapable of making those decisions for themselves.

Once you have as much information about your parents' overall situation, begin assessing your options. For example, if it is clear that living alone is detrimental to your parents' health and safety, the obvious option is to try to move them into some form of assisted living. Is that even an option, though? Can they afford it? Are there openings at facilities nearby? A consultation with a geriatric care manager is a good place to begin. Set aside the question of whether or not your parents would agree to move for now. Spend some time researching assisted-living facilities in their city, and make an appointment with one or two of them to explore this option. (For resources on locating assisted-living facilities, helpful professionals, and other services, see appendix B.)

Note to Parents

It is important to have this discussion with your children as well as your health care providers. Talking with your children about these different options will make all of you feel better when and if these decisions need to be made. Again, your children will often seek approval and would prefer it in advance of anything happening to you when you might become incapacitated. Like young children, they long to do the right thing and will look to you for guidance. Middle-aged or not, they are still your children, and they still want to do things with your blessing. Talking to them will also help ease any guilt they might be experiencing with their decisions. Think of this as another gift to your children.

For a variety of reasons, moving your parents to an assisted-living center may not be possible. If you are in this situation, and you are still concerned about leaving your parents in their home alone, don't despair; you still have options. If your primary concern is their health—whether they are taking their medicines and tending to their physical and hygiene needs—a home health care nurse, a trained medical professional who will visit them weekly to monitor their overall health, may be all they need. This is especially helpful if either of your parents has chronic conditions such as diabetes, high blood pressure, heart problems, emphysema, or cancer. The nurse will also check their supply of medications to make sure they are taking them and order more if they run out. He or she will contact your parents' primary-care physician if they need further treatment, and you can request that you be contacted as well.

If your parents are no longer able to live by themselves in their own home and assisted-living facilities are not available or preferred, you may want to arrange twenty-four-hour, live-in care for your parents, if it is financially feasible. If finances do not permit this, then you may consider having them live with you as a possible solution. However, before you make arrangements to have your elderly parents move in with you, please keep in mind the following:

- Discuss with them a long-term plan if their health continues to decline. Coming up with a plan B is always a good idea.
- As their medical condition advances, new options should also be considered for additional medical care. Their health care providers and geriatric care managers will be a big help to you with this issue.
- Remember that there may come a time when the medical care your parents need is beyond your ability to give, and they may require

professional care in a facility. An example would be if they fall, and you, the caregiver, lack the strength to pick them up or bathe them, especially if they cannot help themselves at all.

Your parents may also need assistance with meals and nutrition, and you have several options here. Most communities provide Meals on Wheels or similar services for senior citizens to ensure your parents receive at least one daily nutritious meal. Or you can hire a person to visit your parents on a regular basis to prepare meals that can be refrigerated and easily heated up by one of your parents. Churches, synagogues, and service organizations may be able to provide volunteers to do this.

I know of a family that had several relatives who lived close to their parents, and they took turns preparing meals and doing the grocery shopping for the elderly parents. This actually became a much-anticipated event for the family members. In addition to bringing food and checking on the parents, they brought the grandchildren along, which generally brings a lot of joy to the grandparents and the children. In fact, the more you involve your extended family in the care of your parents, the better you will handle the inevitable issues that arise as your parents decline in health. This same family, who shared the care of their parents when they refused to move into assisted living, had one of the most successful and trouble-free estate dissolutions I've ever heard of when the parents eventually passed away. The lesson here is that the family touch can be a great way to manage the issues you will face with aging parents.

Don't Panic

When you start to notice a decline in your parents' physical or mental health, take a deep breath, step back from the situation, and try to gain the perspective of a helping professional rather than a worried son or daughter. Treat your parents with respect. Unless there is a true health emergency, don't treat it as such.

Looking at each situation objectively and keeping your wits about you are the keys. Whenever I see problems with families who are trying to help their parents, it is usually from overreacting. Your parents are likely to be as frightened and worried as you are. Always try to follow this process when you approach your parents about a concern:

1. State your concern clearly and unemotionally.

2. Ask your parents if they share your concern, and if so, what they would like to do about it.

3. Suggest solutions and offer to help.

4. Remind them that you love them.

Your parents deserve your respect, and as the roles start to reverse, they need to see that you have their best interests in mind. Do so lovingly.

When It's Time to Move

At some point, whether your parents agree or not, they may need to leave their home. This is one of the most difficult issues to negotiate, and there are no easy answers. Most likely, you will face battles on two fronts: from your parents, who don't want to leave the home they've had for so long, and from one or more of your siblings who don't want to face reality. The best place to start, as you've heard me say before, is to empathize—to put yourself in your parents' and siblings' shoes and understand why they are so resistant. While it's true that our parents' generation tends to have a stubborn, independent streak, they also have a strong attachment to the memories they experienced in their home.

As for your siblings, they share many of the same fears your parents do; plus, they may not have seen what you have seen. I know of a situation where the last surviving parent was in the early stages of Alzheimer's. On some days she was her old self, clearly lucid with a wonderful sense of humor and able to still put out a great spread at dinnertime. But on other days, she was obviously lost in a fog of dementia, not recognizing her daughter or forgetting she had started to boil potatoes on the stove. The daughter who lived close by and visited regularly saw those bad days, while the daughter who lived several hours away always happened to visit on the good days. Of course, she thought her sister was exaggerating with her claims that Mom was losing it and didn't support any effort to encourage Mom to move into a nearby retirement home.

If you're certain one or both of your parents need to leave the family home for a safer, supervised environment, take a deep breath and consider the feelings of those who resist it. That will at least improve your own attitude and affect your response if you run into resistance.

So how do you broach this subject with your siblings? I recommend, if at all possible, you get everyone else in the family on the same page first. In chapter 1, I recommended keeping a log or journal, recording specific dates and behaviors to demonstrate the decline you have observed. Now is the time to use it. If you did your homework, it will look something like this:

2/7/07	Visited Mom. Back door left open. Mom didn't know me.
2/11/07	Mom called. Said Dad was divorcing her. (Dad has been dead for years.)
2/15/07	Visited Mom. Her old self again. Fun!
2/19/07	Visited Mom. Asked me if I was her sister.
2/23/07	Visited Mom. Found multiple subscriptions to the same magazine.
3/2/07	Police called. Found Mom several miles from her home.
3/8/07	Took Mom shopping. Had a great time. She remembered Tim's birthday.

Arrange to meet with your siblings and show them your journal. Seeing specific behaviors spelled out in black and white is hard to argue with, and once it settles in that your parent may be unsafe if left in the home, your siblings will usually join you in your efforts to seek alternative housing better suited to your parents' needs.

Assuming everyone in the family agrees that your parents need to move, how do you make it happen when they clearly do not want to go? The first step is to proceed just as you did when you tried to get them to make out a will: gentle persistence. Ideally, you want your parents to come to the same conclusion that you have and feel empowered to make the decision themselves. Reason with them. Take them to visit different senior-living facilities to get them interested in all they have to offer. If you are persistent and avoid getting angry or pushy, your parents may see the advantages and agree to move. Don't expect them to be happy about it, and be prepared for some good old-fashioned guilt to be laid on you. By the way, most senior facilities have waiting lists for as long as twelve to thirty-six months, so plan accordingly by meeting with the facility well in advance of this conversation with your parents.

However, you may go through all of these steps I've outlined for you, and you may have executed them perfectly, but your parents still adamantly refuse to move out of the family home. I would highly recommend talking to a geriatric care professional who can assess the situation and offer advice to the family, including your parents. Keep in mind that you always have options, and a professional who works with these situations every day can be of enormous assistance.

Remember Steve and Debbie earlier in the chapter? They eventually had to move Debbie's parents against their will. Both parents were seriously incapacitated and unable to keep up with the demands of living in their home, but they refused to consider moving. Steve and Debbie tried everything and grew increasingly frustrated with her parents because they knew what could happen if they stayed in their home.

One day Steve and Debbie brought her parents to an attractive assisted-living center, walked them to an apartment they had already reserved for them, and the rest is history. It would have gone so much easier on *everyone* if Debbie's parents had arrived at that decision on their own, but because they did not, they unknowingly created great difficulty in everyone's lives. Surprisingly, their parents really didn't protest that much. Perhaps they just needed that nudge to do what even they must have known was necessary. I am certainly not recommending you use this stealth approach, but I know of others who have resorted to similar strategies.

We all know our parents will someday be gone. But when we see them growing weaker, we are flooded with many emotions. One of the biggest and most debilitating is guilt, especially if you have to decide some of the things I've mentioned in this chapter. Many of my clients let things go for too long because they feel so guilty about even thinking about clearing out some of the clutter or moving their parents into a safer environment. If you are feeling guilty right now about the action you need to take, consult someone who can counsel you and your family along the way. Your emotions are quite normal and part of the process.

What many people don't realize is that most of the retirement and assisted-living communities today are beautiful and bustling with activity and social events. If you can get your parents to try it, most of them end up loving it. They won't have to cook anymore or clean much, for that matter, and the food is usually wonderful, so you know they are well fed! Most of the seniors who live in this environment remain active and engage in trips to the theaters, museums, local events, and even travel abroad.

There is no limit to what your parents can enjoy, and they will be around other seniors who refuse to grow old. Scores of my clients have told me they can't imagine why they sat in a dark, lonely house for so long when they could have been out with others having a great time with little or no worries. They have repeatedly said they are so happy that they simplified their lives.

End-of-Life Care

Eventually, you will face the reality of end-of-life care for your parents. Usually, this comes when the parent lapses into a coma and the attending physician tells you to prepare for the end. Emotionally, this will be one of the more difficult points in your journey, but as with every other situation, being prepared will make it flow more smoothly. For example, you may be asked to what extent medical personnel should go to keep your parent alive, an absolutely awful decision to even consider.

At some point while your parents are living, you need to ask them, "If you are ever in a vegetative state and the doctors say you will not recover, what would you want us to do?" Make sure a health care power of attorney is selected far before it ever gets to this point. Jennifer, my geriatric care manager colleague, recalls an elderly mother, who had been a professional cook and loved to eat fine meals, telling her daughter, "If I cannot enjoy the taste of good food, then my quality of life is over." So when the nursing home wanted to insert a feeding tube when her mother was unconscious and could no longer eat, the daughter refused to allow the feeding tube because she had health care power of attorney and knew she was fulfilling what her mom wanted. If your parents are reasonably healthy but approaching their final years, you owe it to them and to yourself to have that conversation about the what-ifs that may become reality. If you and your parents have prepared for those eventualities, you will both benefit.

Helping your parents have the best environment and adding quality of life for their final years is the right thing to do.

What Do I Do Now?

Current situation: when it becomes apparent your mom and dad need extra help.

☑ *Review your diary.* Look for patterns or incidents that concern you.

☑ *Take excess clutter with you.* Each time you visit your parents, take at least one box or bag of old newspapers, magazines, and empty containers.

☑ *Research resources.* Use the resources listed in appendix B or your parents' Yellow Pages (look under *Geriatric Care Managers, Senior Citizens' Organizations*, and *Senior Citizens' Services*) to find potential resources to assist you and your parents. Or search for these resources on the Internet.

☑ *Obtain power of attorney.* Ask your parents if they have selected a power of attorney and health care power of attorney in the event they should become incapacitated.

Five

The Hearse Doesn't Have a Trailer Hitch

Jan called me long after the funeral of her mother. Her dad had passed away twelve years ago, and her mom had lived alone in a cozy house near my hometown. Jan was matter-of-fact when she asked me to conduct an estate sale at her mother's house, and I agreed to meet her there for a consultation.

I parked my car in front of the tidy yard festooned with neatly manicured hedges lining the front of the house and window boxes of colorful perennials, walked through the open front door, and found Jan sobbing on a couch. Knowing that returning to the family home after a funeral can be emotionally taxing, I sat next to her, put my hand on her shoulder, and tried to reassure her.

"I know this is hard, Jan, but we'll get through it," I spoke softly.

"Oh, but you don't understand, Julie," she replied. "Mom's been gone for years. I just can't get myself to let go. Everything I see has so many memories."

I looked around and had to agree that her mom had some lovely things. But in addition to the figurines and framed family photos, on every counter, coffee table, and windowsill were stacks of what I can only call *stuff*. Hundreds of Christmas cards stuffed into a large basket next to the fireplace. Years of subscriptions to *McCall's*, *Good Housekeeping*, *Family Circle*, and other magazines stacked neatly beneath the picture window looking out on the front yard. I opened the coat closet in the foyer and found it stuffed with dozens of winter coats, probably two dozen shoes and boots, and enough hats to start a haberdashery. Just in the kitchen alone I found 23 empty and neatly stored mayonnaise jars, 103 cans of string beans, 41 empty coffee cans, and a drawer filled with nothing but the plastic caps to milk cartons. We also found 77 pencil nubs, 43 notepads, a cluster of bread twister ties the size of a baseball, 17 sour cream containers, and at least 70 keys to unknown locks. Every tabletop in the house had so much on it you couldn't see the table. But the attic was the real surprise. Apparently her husband had built a type of structure that looked like a greenhouse. Inside were boxes of old clothing—more than a thousand sweaters, blouses, slacks, dresses, hats, shoes, gloves, and purses, all carefully protected by the structure.

I turned to Jan, who every now and then would begin crying again as we saw a particular item. "Why don't you pick out your last remaining items and take them out to your car?" I suggested. "I'll continue with my evaluation." She had already brought home so much, and it was causing marital strife, all because she couldn't let go. It was difficult to watch her struggle with taking more and more items home with her.

Jan looked at me as if I were the Grim Reaper. "I don't think I can do it. Maybe I'm not ready for the sale. Maybe it's too soon. [It was three years since her mother's death.] I just can't part with any of this. I want to take it all home with me. Mom's hands touched everything in this house, and it's almost like I'm betraying her if I sell these things; she loved them so much. I will feel so bad if I do this."

From my side of the fence, my clients are usually relieved when they see that all their parents' belongings have found a new home. Some of the items go to those less fortunate. Most parents would not have a problem with that. Other items are sold in an appropriate manner, such as an estate sale, and I tell my clients the one thing they do not see at an estate sale is the happiness on the buyers' faces when they find something they will cherish. These items will make new memories for new people. I encourage my clients who have difficulty letting go that this is a good way to think about this painful issue. The objective here is to empty the home to prepare for the sale of the real property. Once boomers see the home empty, it certainly tugs at their heartstrings, but they know this is part of their responsibility and feel like a huge burden has been lifted. Secretly, boomers *all* wish their moms and dads had done this painful part for them.

I eventually convinced Jan that she was doing the right thing, and I even got her husband's assistance in supporting her, especially the day of the estate sale. Jan did feel better after the sale. However, as my assistant and I were packing things up for donation postsale, Jan kept pulling things out of the donation boxes to "give to family." She *still* couldn't let go.

This happens more often than you think, and it may happen to you as well. In this chapter, I will help you understand why your parents held on to everything and how you can successfully break the cycle and not leave *your* kids with this burden. Since no one can take it with them when they leave this earth, you must make responsible plans for your assets.

The Generation that Never Threw *Anything* Out

Though I have helped hundreds of boomers clean out their parents' estates, the majority of my clients lived through the Depression era. This particular generation rarely disposes of much, thinking in terms of what can be used later or perhaps increase in value through the years. They are very practical, and that is a good thing . . . until the accumulation gets out of hand. Generally, they hold on to items so long, the items are no longer useful. By then, the accumulation has reproduced like rabbits in the closets, attic, garage, and basement. Over the course of time, the situation becomes overwhelming. So they often assume their children will take care of it when they die because they had to deal with their parent's accumulation when they died. There are some really big differences between this generation and boomers.

For starters, our parents' generation kept most of the previous generation's property and accumulation because it was sentimental or perceived as family heirlooms. Stories were handed down that a certain item belonged to their great-great grandfather in 1837. (As an appraiser, this is the part where I have to say they had junk in 1837 too. Just because it is old does not mean it is valuable . . . more on that in chapter 9.)

So here you have not only your mom and dad's accumulation, but you have absorbed your grandmother and grandfather's belongings as well as stuff from Aunt Martha and Great-Uncle Joe. Instead of just one generation, you are now dealing with several or somewhere between 70 and 150 years of accumulation.

But there is more to the picture. The children of the Greatest Generation, the baby boomers, lead totally different lives than our parents did. We work far from home and often travel across the globe, raise our families while working, are often geographically remote to our parents, and generally do not have the same sense of sentimentality that previous generations did. Boomers do not have expendable time. This new equation leads to a dilemma that most have not yet begun to think about, and it is a far greater issue than we realize.

Which leads me to this question: how long has it been since you spent some time in your parents' home? I don't mean just visiting them but walking through the basement or climbing up into the attic. Have you opened any of the closets, looked in the garage or basement? If not, you may be in for a shock. I've seen it so many times—upon visiting the parents' home with clients for the first time, they are completely overwhelmed and can't believe all the stuff that's been tucked away in every nook and cranny over the years. I've seen it all, and there doesn't seem to be any logical reason for the types of things people hold on to. Here's just a small list of the types of things I've found in virtually every home I've been hired to help clear out:

- *Plastic containers.* Every home I've cleaned out has tons of plastic containers! For some reason, the container of choice seems to be Cool Whip, but margarine, cottage cheese, and sour cream containers are also in abundance.

- *Glass containers.* Running a close second to the plastic containers are canning jars, baby food jars, tomato sauce jars, and empty peanut butter and mayonnaise jars. I believe this generation actually initiated the birth of the stackable container organization industry.

- *Magazines and mail-order catalogs.* Hundreds of periodicals and catalogs are usually stacked somewhere as a tripping hazard or laden with mildew if kept in the basement or garage.

- *Nails, nuts, and bolts.* Rusted or not, every size, shape, and type of hardware are stuffed into those coveted baby jars, mayonnaise jars, coffee cans, and canning jars.

- *Used bread twister ties.* (My personal favorite.) I've found literally hundreds of thousands of bread twister ties in my career.

- *Rubber bands, paper clips.* How many rubber bands and paper clips do you really need?

- *Girdle clips.* A painful reminder for all women, this relic from the early to mid-twentieth century has survived in dresser drawers and trinket boxes.

- *Coupons.* Drawers stuffed with outdated coupons and coupon books. Some of the products don't even exist anymore.

- *Medicine.* Most homes I clean out have enough medicines to start a pharmacy, some dating back fifty years. Caution: this is dangerous! Medicine must be destroyed after the expiration date. Call your local pharmacy or dissolve pills completely in a half-vinegar and half-water solution; then flush them. (Vinegar neutralizes medicines.) Never flush undissolved medicines or throw them out. There are people who rummage through garbage who could get sick from them, and you certainly don't want medicines getting in the water supply.

- *Flowerpots.* Homes and garages filled with clay, porcelain, plastic, cracked, chipped, and fractured flowerpots of all varieties.

- *Grocery bags.* You know, when the cashier asks you "Paper or plastic?" at the grocery store? This generation says, "Both." We find a lifetime supply of grocery bags in nearly 85 percent of all estates. Some bags are so old they disintegrate in your hands.

- *Canned goods.* We find hundreds of canned goods, most of them beyond their expiration date. Some are swollen with age, seeping, and stuck to the shelf, attracting unwanted pests. Donate in-date canned goods to your local food bank or shelter if your parents will not consume them. Food that is beyond its expiration date is extremely hazardous to anyone's health. Dispose of it immediately.

- *Paint cans.* Good paint should be saved for the new homeowner for any touch-up work. Ancient paint from the original color of the house in the 1950s is no longer good and is beyond its usability. Dispose of it appropriately in the chemical section at the local dump.

- *Hats and clothing.* I could easily trace many fashions back to the Roaring Twenties or before, but most of it was kept in the attic and, therefore, eaten by moths, stained, and of little value.

- *Reader's Digest Condensed Books.* By the thousands. No one seems to want these books, so we donate them to local charities.

- *Jewelry.* Costume and genuine jewelry but mostly large collections of costume. Back in their day, the ladies loved being color-coordinated with their purses, shoes, hats, and jewelry. Costume jewelry can have significant value and is sought after by collectors. Genuine jewelry needs to be appraised.

- *Photos and home movies.* In most homes, we find boxes upon boxes of slide carousels and thousands of slides. It is sad, but most kids do not take the time to go through them and usually dispose of them. This time-consuming endeavor does not generally appeal to boomers and their rapidly paced lifestyles.

- *Rock and shell collections.* Many of these collections may be broken or crumbled from boxes that have been stacked on them for years in the attic.

- *Old radios, TVs, and other outdated technologies.* Since this generation has lived through tremendous technological changes, it is not uncommon to find old console stereos and black-and-white TVs, cassette and eight-track tapes, transistor radios, record players, rotary telephones, or parts thereof. Some are collectible; others are disposable.

- *Books.* Many estates have fifty-year-old high school and college textbooks, everything from typewriter maintenance to early-twentieth-century accounting. Most are obsolete.

Boxes and Bags and Piles, Oh My!

Many people in this country, regardless of age, collect something and have a tendency to accumulate and keep things they don't really need. Our parents' generation has simply had many more years to accumulate. However, the quantity of what they have kept often surprises us, not necessarily for the better.

To the boomer child, it may not make sense to keep collections like this. And I'm not talking about a little box of this or that, but boxes and bags and piles sometimes stacked to the ceiling. Why in the world did your parents keep all this stuff, and what are you going to do with it? I have spent years trying to understand the mind-set of this generation, and I think it goes something like this:

- *I just never know when I'm going to need it.*
- *There are so many things I could use it for.*
- *I had to go without as a kid, so I will never go without again.* (Since we didn't experience the Great Depression, we cannot comprehend what they lived through and need to respect this sentiment.)
- *It was a gift, and I will honor the giver by keeping it.*
- *If I hold on to it long enough, it might become valuable.*
- *All old things are valuable.*
- *The more I leave the kids, the more they will have.*

Let's try to understand the world your parents grew up in. If your parents are in their seventies or eighties, they lived through the Great Depression and know what it's like to go without. A pencil was something sharpened down to the stub, used repeatedly, and then saved in a drawer because they didn't have the two cents to buy a new one. They canned vegetables grown in their victory gardens, and if they didn't use an entire bottle of a prescription drug, they saved a few pills to avoid having to pay for a new one should their sore throats return. Having gone through those hard times when a vibrant economy collapsed, they became forever suspicious that it could happen again. So if the corner A&P had a sale on canned green beans, they bought a case and stored them in the basement to get ahead of the game when the next depression came along: *I'm never going to without again.* And who could blame them?

This generation gave us the slogan "waste not, want not," which explains why they kept that can of paint after using three-fourths of it to paint the front porch. I don't know how many bags and boxes of little slivers of bars of soap I've found, but it makes sense when you get inside your parents' minds: *If we can't afford to buy a bar of soap, we've got all these little nibs that will work just fine.* Throwing things away just wasn't an option.

Interestingly enough, even though they believe in waste not, want not, this generation is responsible for considerable waste (not everyone, of course, but some). Using some of my earlier common examples of food gone bad, we can add to that 22 pairs of manicuring scissors, 8 boxes of Band-Aids, 17 tubes of toothpaste, 12 cans of hair spray, 9 dishwasher detergents, 6 bottles of bleach, 7 bottles of shampoo, 15 bedsheets not used since the '60s, and finally, 3 French hens, 2 turtledoves, and a partridge in a pear tree. (I find those too!)

You can see where I am going with this. Many of these things have been sitting on shelves for a decade and are no longer usable. Since no one has used them, and they were not donated for someone to use them, this *is* waste.

Your parents bought and kept all of these things with the best of intentions, thinking they would use them at some point. Maybe they forgot these things were in the cupboard and went out and bought more. Maybe they forgot they had all those scissors. It happens. It happens to us too.

Note to Parents

I am not intending to come down hard on you, but I am painting a realistic picture of what I see in most estates. Many people are guilty of buying an item and forgetting where they put it, so they buy another. Sometimes I think people get so overwhelmed by all they have to clean out, they just give up! But please do not give up. Remember, it took you years to accumulate these things, and it will take some time to clear them out. This process will go more quickly if you get help. Whatever you do, please do not leave it for your children to contend with. If you are overwhelmed by all your belongings, just imagine how your children will feel, especially in the midst of an already emotional situation.

Getting Rid of It Is Harder than You Think

My point here is that your folks weren't crazy for keeping all that stuff, even if it's driving *you* crazy trying to figure out what to do with it, and that presents an even bigger problem. Believe it or not, you're going to have just as hard a time getting rid of all that stuff as your parents had. In the days and weeks following the loss of your last surviving parent, everything your mom or dad touched will carry with it a reminder and become an extension of his or her life. I recall a gentleman who ran across a box of his dad's old cuff links. These were in bad condition, with gold plating worn off and stones missing, but he wanted to keep them. "Dad always wore these cuff links to work and on Sunday to church," he explained. "I can remember it so clearly, just like when I was a boy. I just can't let them go."

You don't need *things* to remember your mom or dad or another loved one. Just close your eyes and check in with your heart. It is there you will find that loved one.

It has been my experience that the older boomer is far more sentimental than the younger boomer. And the younger generations, X and Y, seem to want very little or nothing but the cash proceeds from the real property. They really don't care much for Grandma's stuff. Sad but true, most grandmas who are clients of mine are well aware of this fact, and it does trouble them. They realize there is nothing they can do about it and eventually accept it because they are so gracious. The younger generations, boomers included, are accustomed to a life of change and luxury. The furniture and décor in our homes change frequently just because our tastes have changed. Not so in our parents' generation. They bought a sofa to last sixty-five years. Today that thought would never occur to most of us.

While it is important to keep one or two items that have only sentimental value, you should resist the temptation to keep your parents' memories alive by keeping all of their stuff. After all, the memories will always be there, ready to recall at any moment. Realistically, if you keep these types of things, you will probably put them in a box, store it somewhere, and never take them out to revisit the good times you had with your parents. And you know what? Someone else—probably your own kids—will have to deal with those boxes someday.

On a side note, many of my clients regret taking too much, only to call me a year or two later to come get the items and sell them because it has caused too much marital stress due to the clutter in their own home.

Fast Facts

- The average household purchases 13,000 bags of stuff in a year.
- On average, a woman spends 55 minutes each day searching for things.
- 80 percent of what we keep we never use.
- The average household has 25 percent more furniture and 75 percent more things than they need.
- Each of the 293,000 letter carriers employed by the U.S. Postal Service delivers 17.8 tons of bulk mail annually.
- The average American buys 6.7 pairs of shoes a year.
- Americans use 14 billion plastic shopping bags annually.
- 80 percent of the things placed in home file cabinets are never referenced again.[1]

There's another reason that it's hard to part with the variety of stuff your parents leave behind, and that's the possibility that there might be something valuable in that collection and you don't want to donate something that is worth thousands of dollars. So your initial thought will be to put everything in storage until you can go through it piece by piece and salvage those valuables. Here's the sobering reality: while it is true that treasure might be hiding in attics and basements all over America and some estates do produce higher-end items, more often than not, the average estate is filled with good usable items, not necessarily priceless treasures. Rather than cart everything off to your own basement, hire a professional appraiser to go through the house and identify anything of value. It's worth the extra cost and will save unnecessary "holding on to" on your part. Plus, it is the only way to know for sure that you've identified any valuables, granting you peace of mind. A professional appraiser may even uncover something of value that you might have thrown away or donated by accident. I've found that most of my customers keep the antique furniture, thinking it is valuable because it is old, and they toss out other good items. Remember, just because it is old doesn't mean it is valuable. (I'll go into greater deal on this in chapter 9.)

Quick Decisions for Cleaning Out the Clutter

1. *Everything plastic and paper gets recycled.* There's absolutely no reason to keep plastic bags, margarine or Cool Whip containers, or anything made out of plastic.

2. *Dress the less fortunate.* Empty everything in the wardrobe and donate to homeless shelters or charity.

3. *No serious treasure in the kitchen.* Pots and pans, casserole dishes, utensils, toasters, Dutch ovens, even dishes and glassware—you don't need them, so don't waste any time in getting rid of them.

4. *If it's been opened, it goes.* Food items, cans of paint, cleaning products, medicine bottles, cosmetics—if they've been opened, toss them. For anything toxic or chemical, check with a refuse company on how to dispose safely. Your local dump may have a section just for chemicals.

5. *Old news is bad news.* There is little demand for old newspapers and magazines like *National Geographic* or *Woman's Day.* Today, most of these can be found online. Consider recycling. However, if you have found the April 29, 1865, edition of *Harper's Weekly* announcing the assassination of President Lincoln, it may have a value of about $600 if in good condition, and I certainly would not toss it!

6. *Old Spice, no dice.* All personal toiletries or products can go straight to the trash unless the products are still unused and can be donated. Remember to dissolve medications in vinegar and water; then flush.

7. *Banish the books.* Books generally sell for a dollar or two apiece. The paperbacks are most difficult to sell, so we just donate them. Another option may be to call your local library to ask if they are taking book donations. If you are in a smaller community, they might accept books, but some libraries are filled to the brim with books and will have an annual book sale. Even a good many antique books are not valuable. However, an appraiser should look through them to make sure. Antique leather-bound books are usually sought after by collectors.

The Ugly Painting over the Mantel

I received a phone call from a gentleman in Oregon whose parents' home was in my hometown. "Both of my parents have died, and I need to clear out their house," he told me. "I have no idea what things are worth, but I'm guessing it's all stuff for donation. Could I buy an hour or two of your time for you to take a look and put my mind at ease that I'm not getting rid of anything valuable?"

Smart man. For the most part, he was absolutely right. It was a modest home with well-worn furniture and the usual collection of knickknacks. But as I walked from the kitchen into the living room, I noticed a painting above the fireplace mantel. It wasn't very appealing, but I recognized the artist's name and noted the price on the back of $1,500 dated in 1949. That was a lot of money back then, so I decided to do a little research and informed the son I would get back to him. He laughed and told me how everyone in the family hated that painting and felt their parents had gotten taken by some slick salesman. "I'd be thrilled if you could get me what they paid for it, but I'm not holding my breath," he laughed.

I went back to my office and begin researching the painting and discovered it would probably bring a minimum of six figures. I just love making those phone calls! After he recovered from the surprise, I gave him the appropriate resources to sell the painting and wished him luck. About a year later he called me to report they had found a buyer and sold the painting for well over $100,000, and he thanked me profusely for helping him put his kids through college. I had to wonder if the painting was suddenly more likable now (and secretly wondered if he ever told the rest of the family; I certainly hope so).

It's Not All Junk!

Do not be hasty in throwing everything out because you are in a rush. Hire a professional, and know the facts of what is in the house. It is worth taking a little bit of extra time to do so. Here's why.

A while back, I met with a daughter in her fifties who really didn't want to go through the process of dissolving her parents' estate. According to her, it was "all junk." My usual comment to this type of person is, "Well, we all have some junk, but your parents have some keepers, I am sure. We just have to find them, and that's my job."

I ordered a Dumpster for the attic debris with the intention of using it only for that purpose. My instructions to her were very clear: "Do not throw anything away until I get there tomorrow morning at eight o'clock. My assistant and I will sift through it all and know what to do with everything." When we arrived at the house the very next morning, the Dumpster was at least half-full. Being rather short statured, I got up on my tiptoes and peered in the Dumpster and suddenly felt a lump in my throat. "Do you know what that is?" I shouted to my client as I pointed to what looked to her I'm sure like an old box. "It's a turn-of-the century Louis Vuitton trunk in fabulous condition!"

Throwing myself over the side and into the Dumpster, I opened the trunk. Inside, I found tons of World War II photos, two uniforms, bayonets, war medals, and the like. Needless to say, the daughter was overjoyed when later I sold the trunk for $4,100, and the contents sold for an additional $1,200. Not a bad Dumpster find if I do say so myself.

Use caution when throwing things away. I promise you, it is not all junk.

My point here is that there is a right way and a wrong way to determine what to do with all that stuff your parents have been collecting. Chances are there are no $100,000 paintings hanging on the walls of your parents' home. Most likely, there are items, perhaps a decorative piece that might be worth several times what your parents paid, yet those are the things that *often* get carted off to the Dumpster or are donated. There's even a bigger chance that the silverware and jewelry you are banking on are considerably less in value than you realize.

Your ultimate goal is to empty the house without adding to your own stacks of stuff. Remember, the more you take, the more *your* kids will have to contend with. The panic you feel when you discover just how much your parents have collected will soon pass. The process I describe in the next few chapters will enable you to get through this in a wise and efficient manner, but for now, we need to get past the immobilization most people feel when they step into their parents' home for the first time after their passing.

Not Just Your Parents' Clutter

As I said before, however, this isn't just an older adult problem. *All* of us are holding on to too much stuff. Have you noticed the number of rentable storage facilities in your area? They're all over the place. Did you know that the self-storage industry is the fastest growing sector of the commercial real estate business? It's a $22 billion business and growing every year. In 1995, one out of seventeen households rented storage space. In 2007, the number had climbed to one in ten households. And it's not that we don't have enough rooms in our homes. The average size of a home in the United States in 1974 was 1,695 square feet. Today it's 2,500 square feet and getting bigger. More than 51,000 self-storage rental businesses cover the landscape, providing 2.2 billion square feet of storage space—that's bigger than New York City's entire island of Manhattan![2] Guess who's storing their stuff there? Not your parents, but people like you and me. What other reason would launch television programs like The Learning Channel's *Clean Sweep*?

As you face the task of clearing out your parents' estate, this might be a good time to take a look into your own closets and attic. Even though the majority of my clients are baby boomers who need me to help clear out their parents' estates, I've also had to liquidate an occasional estate of someone much younger, and I have to reluctantly admit that it's not just old people who have accumulated a lot of stuff. Maybe it's in our DNA, but all of us seem to develop an emotional attachment to things.

Many of our own homes have begun to fill up with all sorts of items we don't really need. In fact, just as we don't want to get rid of our parents' stuff because we cling to the memories they represent, I believe we're holding on to our kids' old toys and schoolwork because we think it takes some of the emptiness out of the empty nest. I know of one middle-aged mother who has a basement full of all her now-grown kids' sports equipment, and it's not because they want it or she plans to use it. Those baseball cleats and soccer uniforms remind her of the days when her home was filled with laughing, rambunctious children, and she wants to hold on to those memories. Well, she'll always have the memories and doesn't really need boxes and plastic bags to trip over when she does the laundry.

The truth is boomer children are well-established in their work and finances, and the same goes for our homes. Our homes are already full of stuff! If you are married, then you and your spouse each have your own stuff. The next thing you know, everyone has too much stuff, and stuff in general becomes a thorn in everyone's paw. Then you have to deal with your mom and dad's stuff when they become infirm or pass away, and everyone knows that your parents' stuff includes your grandparents' stuff. Suddenly, stuff has now been elevated from a thorn in the paw to a real pain in the rear. Going through your mom and dad's estate, you realize what I have said all along: there's more than one generation of stuff here. Suddenly, you have to figure out what all the stuff actually is, how much it is worth, and what to keep, throw away, or donate. *And heaven help me, where do I begin?* (For more on how you can simplify and declutter your home, see chapter 13.)

I don't want to sound judgmental because I'm including myself here, but after spending close to twenty years crawling over piles of stuff from wonderful, decent, mostly middle-class Americans, I think we may be trying to substitute possessions for the real thing. And even though we've all heard the adage, "You can't take it with you," we seem to be trying to hold on to our belongings until the last second, just in case. But as the title of this chapter points out, I've never seen a hearse pulling a trailer.

What Do I Do Now?

Current situation: your parents can no longer keep up with their house, and it is filled with clutter.

- ☑ *Hire a property appraiser.* An appraiser can identify items of value in your parents' belongings. Make a list and keep it for later use.

- ☑ *Clean up your own house.* By the end of the week, appropriately dispose of at least ten items stored in your attic, garage, or basement.

- ☑ *Find a charity.* Locate a charitable organization of your choice or an agency that works with the homeless who would make use of donated items from your parents' home. Many of them will come to the house and pick them up.

Six

Relatively Speaking

One of the most difficult challenges I face when I am hired to liquidate an estate is the exploitation of the deceased. It's absolutely heartbreaking. Often, even as the homeowner is slowly slipping away with death only days away, someone is rifling through drawers or sneaking into closets to take whatever he or she wants. Wouldn't it be wonderful if we could keep Mr. Plunder and Miss Pillage out of the picture? I'd like to say this is the exception, but it happens with unbelievable predictability.

The saddest reality of this exploitation is that you must *expect* it in order to beat it. The faces of exploitation are often familiar faces of friends, neighbors, or family members. Remember my earlier story of the woman with Alzheimer's and how her neighbors and friends made off with the heirlooms? Even in close-knit and apparently caring families, sinister behavior creeps in when an aging parent dies. My mother always said you can spot a person's true colors when a loved one dies, and she is right. In this chapter, I will help you see how this happens and give you strategies for preventing it.

When Good Relatives Do Bad Things

Before I share some of my stories, I want to remind you of the types of clients I work with because when you hear some of my stories, you might think they are fictional. I can assure you they are not. The typical clients I work with are middle- to upper-middle-class families who live in nice neighborhoods and are respectable citizens. Most are active in their communities, synagogues, and churches and share memories of joyful family reunions, holiday gatherings, and family vacations. I walk through their homes and see pictures on the mantel of smiling children and go through boxes of greeting cards with loving notes of appreciation. These are decent people like you and me who probably think they are incapable of anything toward their families but kindness and compassion. But as they face the end of an era where they no longer have their moms and dads around, something happens. Exploitation raises its ugly head through suspicion, jealousy, and plain old greed.

Such was the case with a family I will call the Garfields. Dad Garfield was one of the kindest, most generous men you could ever know. A supervisor in a local manufacturing plant, he taught Sunday school at his church and volunteered his free time to help widows with maintenance jobs in their homes. His three adult children lived nearby, and he loved nothing more than to have them bring the grandchildren over for Sunday dinners. All of his kids were successful in their own right, and the family often took vacations together. As Mom Garfield explained to me later, she could not recall a moment of discord between her kids after they had married and started their own families.

Dad Garfield was diagnosed with cancer at age seventy-three, and the disease progressed rapidly. He had lived a good life and faced his illness with grace and courage. Even as his strength waned, he loved having his family visit and was able to sit in the living room and listen to stories of how his grandkids excelled in school. But soon he began slipping fast, and hospice was called to assist him and his family as death was imminent. That's when strange things began to happen.

One of his daughters—we'll call her Sandy—became uncharacteristically possessive. She wanted to be by Dad Garfield's bedside around the clock and got annoyed when her siblings offered to relieve her. Normally a sweet and accommodating person, she would snap at her mother over the smallest things and accuse her siblings of not caring enough for their dad even as she tried to prevent them from being with him during his final days.

Eventually Dad Garfield passed away, his wife and children standing around his hospital bed in the living room of their home. But as the funeral director's hearse pulled up to take the body to the funeral home, Sandy disappeared into the basement while the others comforted one another in their grief. It was a few days later that they discovered what she had been doing. Apparently, while she was keeping vigil by her father's bedside, she was also surveying his belongings. When he died, Sandy quickly grabbed the things she had stashed in the last couple of weeks. Mysteriously, even though Dad Garfield had prepared a will, it was never found.

Note to Parents

This is a scary story, no doubt. But imagine, for just a moment, how different this story would have gone if the parents had given serious consideration to dividing their estate prior to infirmity or death. Or, at the very least, if they had distributed a master list of what they wanted each child or heir to have, making sure that each child received a copy. If every child knows what is going on, it will be much harder for one child to get the lion's share.

You might think this is a horror story I made up to make a point, but it's true and sadly representative of what I see all too often. It's not even the worst story by far. I've seen siblings shout at each other, push and shove, change the locks on the family home without notifying the others, and all sorts of other shocking behavior. In many cases, siblings argue over something they both want *in front of the parent who is on his deathbed!*

Now here's the good news. I've also seen families go through the tragedy of loss and remain close throughout the entire process of handling the estate. I've seen siblings be very careful to make sure they don't take anything the other wants. In one case, they almost fought to be generous: "You go ahead and take Dad's military medals. I know he would have wanted you to have them," to which his brother replied, "No, you take them. It's okay." This is how it should be: putting your feelings aside to promote peace and well-being in everyone, including yourself.

At the beginning of this chapter, I referred to Mr. Plunder and Miss Pillage and warned you that most of the time, the people who take advantage of or steal from your parents are relatives or someone familiar to you. Now I would like to give you some specific strategies for keeping them at bay.

Know the Plan

Knowledge is power. Just having the facts will reduce all kinds of challenges. It's when you hide things that people start acting irrationally. The more facts you know about your parents' affairs, the less you will have to decide on your own later on. Make sure everyone in the family has talked with them about their estate planning and final wishes. It is imperative you know the following:

- Is there a will?
- Where is the will?
- Where is a copy of the will?
- Is the will updated? (A will should be reviewed every ten years or sooner.) If there is no will, enlist the help of an estate planning attorney (discuss health care issues and trusts as well).
- Do you know who the executor is?
- Do you know who your parents' attorney is?
- Do you know who your parents' financial planner is?
- Do you know what to do if your parents have to move to assisted living?
- Do you know your parents' end-of-life wishes?

Be Fair

When it comes to your parents' estate, everyone must be on the same page at the same time. This means that all siblings must be in the loop. If both parents have died, then the executor is responsible for making sure all of the heirs are informed as to what is happening with the estate.

The executor should keep everyone notified through e-mail or letters, being sure to include everyone *all the time*. Conference calls are okay, as long as everyone is present and accounted for. What you do for one, you must do for the others. This will greatly minimize challenges along the way. I guarantee you that not everyone is going to behave as they should, but at least they will all have the same knowledge, and no one person is selected to know more or have more. No sibling should have the upper hand when it comes to dividing your parents' estate. You will encounter those who possess an entitlement mentality, but do not waver for anyone at any time. This is harder than you think but 100 percent necessary.

Be Honest

Now, as far as making everyone happy, if you do all you can to be as up-front and honest with each other as much as possible, you stand a much better chance of going through the process in an easier fashion. This is not a guarantee that everyone will walk away happy, but it certainly could not hurt the situation. For example, if you have always admired the painting over your parents' bed and think your sister feels the same way, tell her you would really like to have it because you have enjoyed looking at it since you were a kid, which is the truth. She will come back with one of two responses: she likes it and wants it too, or it isn't her taste, so she would prefer you have it. If she wants it too, you will find the answer in chapter 8, the nitty-gritty of dividing your parents' estate.

Be honest about any correspondence or conversation you have had with your parents regarding the disposition of certain items. For example, if your mother mentioned in conversation that she would like your brother's wife to have her set of pearls, please honor her wishes by telling your brother that and making sure he has them when the family gets together to divide the contents of the home. It will impress your brother and make your sister-in-law really happy. This is another example of why it is important to get a master list of who gets what from your parents. If it is documented, there should be no questions or squabbling. But if it was verbal, at least be honest and share that with your siblings.

Be honest about any items in your parents' home that may, in fact, belong to you or one of your siblings. An example of this would be if Rick bought his mom a car, and the other siblings assumed that she purchased the Buick on her own. If Rick can provide proof that he bought the car and gave it to her, is the car rightfully his? If his name is on the title, the car belongs to him. If his mother's name is on the title, the car is considered a completed gift and goes into the estate.

Be honest about what is being taken from the home after the funeral. If Kay, the local daughter, gets to the house first and wants to remove the silver and jewelry from the home to protect it from possible theft while the home is without an occupant, everything must be documented as to who has these items and their current location. Immediate communication is necessary with all siblings. On a personal note, I would never remove anything until after all the siblings agree that they need to be removed. If all siblings agree that these items need to be kept in a safe place, then agree on a location, perhaps a bank safe-deposit box or even at Kay's house for the time being. Remember, this new home for the items is only temporary. Many, many fights erupt over this one issue. I would imagine it is because most families have someone who will rush right over and help themselves before anyone else is there to stop them. This is another good reason to control the keys to the house and get a master list from your parents!

Don't Take It Personally

Let's face it: it's hard not to take it personally when someone else—the executor—is making all the decisions, and you don't agree with something. The executor has a monumental task. He or she requires your help and understanding because this person is in the hot seat until the estate is settled. If the executor has to constantly worry about the sister getting snippy or the brother making off with his father's war medals, this just further complicates and delays the division of the estate.

Choosing an executor should be given careful consideration. It is a very difficult task, and you should choose someone who will get it done in a fair and timely fashion. Here are a couple of things you may or may not know about an executor's responsibilities.

The executor cannot do what he or she wants to do. The executor must follow the provisions of the will, which is called *fiduciary duty* (a legal relationship between two or more parties; the highest standard of care to the person who requested him to serve as his executor). The court oversees and must approve of what the executor has done.

An executor cannot dodge responsibilities. Even if you are disgruntled that your brother was selected as executor instead of you, maybe you should count your lucky stars. Being named an executor carries huge responsibilities that cannot be shirked. In other words, it's a lot of work; the best thing to do if you are not the executor is to support the person who is.

Note to Parents

While this is a most difficult choice, I would recommend selecting an executor who is up for the challenge, not advanced in age, not a procrastinator, and someone who will have your best interests at heart. Don't worry about hurting anyone's feelings. This is your estate, and it must be handled in a manner that is comfortable to you.

Work Cooperatively with One Another

It goes without saying that during this long and difficult process, everyone needs to cooperate. Doing so will promote a much smoother process. You can plan on the fact that someone will throw a nut or bolt into the works. This will naturally clog up the mechanism, but don't let it mess up your relationships. Working as a team will accomplish your goal twice as fast. Playing tug-of-war is tiresome and time-consuming. Remember, too, that ultimately none of this is about you and what you want. It's all about your parents and fulfilling their wishes, whether in life or death.

Document Everything

I can't say this enough—I'm a big believer in putting everything in writing. This is designed to protect all the parties involved.

Protect All Assets

If you are the executor of your parents' estate, you have a responsibility to protect all they owned until decisions have been made about the items' disposal. Here are some practical ways to do this.

Retrieve the keys to your parents' home. This includes neighbors, friends, and, yes, even family members. Things have a way of disappearing, and locks have a way of getting changed. Start with a clean slate, and get back every key if you know where they are, or if you are unsure of the location of the keys, change the locks *with everyone's knowledge*. It is a small price to pay a locksmith for peace of mind.

No one should remove anything from the house immediately after a parent's death. This is common, yet it is a huge mistake families make. This one issue alone causes great disturbances among the children. "Mary took the silver home with her after the funeral," or "John packed up and took all of Dad's antique tools, and we have no idea what they were worth!" This is a big no-no. We are trying to establish a fair playing ground for all involved. If you have to remove items from the home for security reasons, read on.

If you feel an item should be removed for security reasons, have the executor document who has the item and the location of it, and make sure the person understands it is a temporary home only. If you feel it is necessary to have the person sign a receipt for your records, then he or she should understand and *not* take it personally. It is being done for the good of the entire situation. Sometimes a death will signal a vacant house to a thief watching in the neighborhood. So the recommendation would be to remove the estate jewelry, sterling silver, personal legal papers, insurance documents, or anything else of significant value. (Ask your attorney for advice on this.) The recommendation is to keep these things local so the executor can keep track of them, and these items will be present and accounted for during the division of property. Everyone should be aware of who has what until the *day of division*. All items should be brought back to the home prior to the day of division, but please, no excuses. You must bring them.

The more timely the division of personal property with the siblings, the less worry you will have about burglary. Draw the curtains and blinds every time you leave the home, and have a lamp timer to come on in a couple of rooms in the home. Remember to leave the air-conditioning on. Nothing is worse than turning off the utilities and coming back to a house that smells of mildew and seeing mold.

Do Your Best to Work Through this in a Timely Manner

Sometimes there is an allotted period of time in which to settle an estate, especially if a time frame is dictated in the will. But it would be in everyone's best interest to settle everything as fairly and as reasonably as possible in a timely manner. I compare this process to removing a Band-Aid. Pull it off slowly, and it is painful, even torturous. Pull it off with a faster approach, and it will sting but not hurt. Plus, it will be over with!

Many people ask me what's the longest or shortest amount of time I have ever seen in clearing out a parent's home. The longest is twenty-two years. The boomer child was wealthy and could not bear to dissolve the family home. By the time he was ready to let it go, the furniture and paintings were ruined.

The shortest is within a week. Some children will fly in all at the same time of the funeral and clear out the home. As a professional, I can easily do it inside of a week, but that is because appraisers know the most appropriate methods for determining what things are worth. If you follow the process I describe in this book, you, too, will be able to clean up your parents' estate in ten days or less—without any of the good stuff headed to the Dumpster or donation box.

Advice for Managing Relatives

How do you make sure your own family doesn't fight over your parents' belongings? What can you do right now to prepare for the passing of your parents and a peaceful, harmonious distribution of their property? Of course, the best protection against family rivalries is an updated will from your parents (see chapter 3) along with preparation and preplanning with mom and dad.

Here's some additional advice for keeping the peace in your family:

- Encourage your parents to create a wish list of what they want to give and to whom, and distribute copies to every child or heir. This way, everyone has a copy, and if they are unhappy, they have to take it up with the parents while they are still alive.

- Understand that you are not entitled to anything unless someone gives you an inheritance or gift. Your parents can do whatever they want with their estate. Just being their child does not guarantee you an inheritance. If you receive an inheritance, be exceptionally thankful.

- Understand that settling an estate is one of the most difficult things you and your siblings will go through, especially during the division of personal property (more on that in chapter 8). Chances are pretty good you won't be pleased with the outcome of what you walk away with, but be thankful anyway.

- Remember that this is not about you; it's about what your parents want. This is why it is imperative that a last will and testament and other legal documents be drawn up by an attorney, and you should encourage your parents to make decisions prior to infirmity or death.

As you can see, it's all about attitude, and you can set the example for the rest of your family by putting your parents' wishes ahead of your own.

Note to Parents

Parents, remember this one important rule: what you do for one child, you must do for all of them to keep everyone on the same page at the same time. For example, if you offer one child an heirloom worth $5,000, then you must offer your other children or heirs items of equal value or the equivalent amount of cash. And make sure that all of your wishes, are known to all your children or heirs, not just to the executor of your estate, unless you have personal reasons to withhold any of them. By doing so, you are promoting a fair environment for all involved.

Seven Types of Relatives

In my experience working with families, I've come to see at least seven types of relatives. As you read through these different types, ask yourself two questions. First, which one of these relatives are you? Be honest even if it means you have to face up to something undesirable about yourself. I believe anyone can change for the better, but first you have to face your imperfections and acknowledge that you could be the problem. Second, do you see any of your relatives in the following list? Knowledge is power, and if you know what you may be facing, you will be prepared for what may happen in your family.

Here are the seven types of relatives who surface when a parent dies:

Loving relative. Certainly every relative has a capacity to love, and we all want to be known as a loving relative. Happily, this is the majority of people I see in my business. They are what every senior parent hopes all his children will be. When the parent dies, this relative is only concerned about the loss and not with what he or she can get out of it. This is usually the relative who steps forward to tie up all the loose ends and make sure everyone else is comforted. He wants to do only what his deceased parent would want him to do. While this describes most of the relatives with whom I work, it only takes one difficult relative to turn a sorrowful occasion into a nightmare.

Well-meaning relative. This person is loving and caring, but he is usually geographically removed from the parents' home and can't take the time off to help on a long-term basis. However, the well-meaning relative always works cooperatively with the other family members to do the right things at all times.

Estranged relative. This relative had a falling-out with someone in the family and, therefore, has strained relationships with the parents and/or siblings. However, this relative is among the first to show up when it comes time to divide the personal belongings of a deceased parent and insists on being given what he wants. Unless there is a will that specifically designates who gets what, this relative will generally be uncooperative and may even contest the division of assets.

Uninformed relative. When it comes time for dissolving and dividing the parents' estate, this relative just wants someone to come in and get rid of everything as soon as possible. He believes the estate has nothing of value and views all the parents' belongings as junk. If this relative's views prevail, the family is vulnerable to exploitation. As I emphasized earlier, never assume that something is junk. This could be an incredibly costly mistake.

Guilty relative. Different from the estranged relative, the guilty relative had a good relationship with the loved one but for whatever reason did not have as much interaction as he now wishes had been the case. This person also may have been absent during the difficult weeks or months leading up to the parent's death because he didn't know how to handle the situation. This relative will try to be cooperative but often mask resentment for having to help tie up loose ends. He will either act out his anger toward other family members or blame himself for not being there when he was needed. Either way, he could create problems for other family members.

Unappreciative relative. An unappreciative relative does not feel the same way about what the deceased valued in his personal property. This relative feels that what he was given did not reflect what *he* thought he was entitled to, and he will be vocal about his feelings. He has no sentimental or emotional regard for what his parents accumulated and will mock efforts to sort through the belongings for things with sentimental value.

Greedy relative. Every family seems to have someone who wants everything—or at least the lion's share of the most valuable things—and can be aggressive in trying to obtain it all. This relative also tends to be a hoarder himself and cares little about the parents' or siblings' wishes. This is the one who is the most unreasonable and uncooperative in dealings regarding the parents' estate and will most often challenge provisions of the will.

Which One Are You?

Now, which one of these descriptions fits you and why? If your parents are still living, try to imagine you and your siblings meeting for the first time after your parents are gone to discuss what to do with their belongings. If you really do have your eyes on some of the more valuable possessions, and your parents' will does not specify who receives them, can you think of an appropriate way to make your wishes known? Would you respect someone who disregarded everyone else's feelings and just grabbed what she could get? It's perfectly natural to desire an item you have always admired. You stand a far better chance of getting it and still maintaining a loving relationship with your siblings if you are fair and respectful to everyone involved. Remember, after your parents are gone, your siblings are all you have.

No one wants to be the culprit in a difficult distribution of personal property, so if you think you have a tendency to be anyone but the loving relative, now is the time to sort out those feelings, and do your best to keep them in check. And one of the best ways to do that is to have open communication with your other family members. So much strife can be minimized in these situations if all the siblings spend some time together and talk honestly about the difficult journey they are facing.

The best example of this that I have seen is two brothers, Roy and Vance, who sought my counsel after their mom passed away unexpectedly. Both sons were from out of town and flew in to handle the estate, and I watched with delight as these two grown men treated each other with great respect and care, even in the midst of grieving their mom. Often, each would turn to the other and say, "No, I would like you to have it because Mom would want you to have it. You will appreciate it more than I will." They also agreed that if one wanted something of more value, it was okay with the other. Clearly, there were no hard feelings and no signs there ever would be. Not only did these brothers honor each other, but in doing so they honored their mother as well.

After you've identified the type of relative you might be, look over the list again and see if any of your siblings fits one or more of the descriptions. When you examined yourself, I asked you to be honest. Here, I will ask you to be fair. It's always easier to pick out the faults in others, so try to be objective and base your judgment on past experiences and behavior. For example, you may have a sibling who always seemed to need more attention from your parents and assume she will be one of those greedy relatives. Her need for attention may not be driven by selfishness at all but by a sense that she never measured up in her parents' eyes. She's more likely to feel guilt than greed, so it would be unfair and inaccurate to portray her as greedy.

The point of this exercise is not to try to change anyone but simply to be aware of what could happen. And again, having an honest conversation with your siblings before your parents die is important because it may clear up misconceptions you have about one another. If you're feeling guilty because you were unable to assist with the care of your ailing parent, admit it to your siblings, and in most cases they will reassure you that they understand and that you don't have to feel bad about it. That will lessen your tendency to be angry or resentful when the time comes to close out your parents' estate.

Knowing what you might be up against is the first strategy in dealing with potentially difficult relationships with other family members. You can build on this by trying to establish regular communication with your siblings and your parents. If you surveyed managers and supervisors in a business, you would discover that poor communication accounts for most of the problems in that business. Whether it's between employees or with customers or vendors, poor communication results in low productivity, difficult decision making, and other inefficient business practices. The same is true in families—though you probably already know that as you do your best to maintain a strong relationship with your spouse and guide your children. For something that seems so simple, even the best of families struggle occasionally with honest and open communication. But when the subject has to do with the death of a parent, no one likes to talk about it.

If your parents are still living, it would be wonderful if you and your siblings could each find ways to talk with your parents about the future. In chapter 2, I've given you talking points for initiating those conversations. If possible, try to approach these conversations in a lighthearted, casual manner: "Mom, you have so many beautiful things that you've collected over the years. Do you know how honored Sylvia and I would be to inherit those someday?" Often, a casual comment like that will disarm your parent from the natural reluctance to talk about her own mortality and open up truly meaningful and ongoing dialogue. I know of one older gentleman who is always humorously "disinheriting" his children. If a son beats him on the golf course, he scolds, "That's it, Jimmy. You're out of the will!" That kind of healthy kibitzing offers an opportunity to respond slightly more seriously: "Oh, Dad, you'll probably outlive all of us, but just for the record, I sure hope you and Mom really have written your wills."

My point here is that there's a right way and a wrong way to communicate about future events, and you will find a more receptive audience in your parents if you avoid sounding demanding or overly urgent. If you pay attention, you will discover opportunities to talk lovingly with your parents about the future, or perhaps they will come to you.

Mom and Dad's Special Gift

My brother and I were lucky. Our parents came to *us*.

Forgive me if I brag a little here, but my mom and dad—Anne and Bill—gave my brother and me the most wonderful gift, one that I wish each of you could receive from your parents. In fact, I hope this book will help you accomplish that wish.

My parents, brother, and I live in different states far from each other. One day while I was visiting my parents, Mom and I were talking casually about the future, and she disappeared into her bedroom. She asked me to come in and sit down beside her on the bed, and then she proceeded to go through a large notebook, page by page. This notebook explained everything, from where she and Dad kept their trust to locations of assets, phone numbers, financial information, even the songs they wanted sung at their funerals. Mom presented this information with such dignity and grace that what could have been an awkward moment became a very natural and comfortable conversation about a difficult subject. Even if my brother or I were a greedy relative, it would make no difference. We both already know exactly who inherits what and are so relieved that everything has already been arranged. But this might not have happened had my parents not had the insight and inclination to take charge of the inevitable and, therefore, greatly minimize the burden on us after they are gone. Talk about love!

I don't know if Mom was uncomfortable sharing that information with me because death is never easy to talk about. I'm not sure she even realized I was trying to fight back tears, sitting on the bed and listening to all of this. Knowing her, she probably had a hunch. As she was talking so matter-of-factly about the end of their lives, my imagination suddenly took over, and I was taken to a place in the future I did not want to think about.

It was a tough conversation. But was it worth it? You bet. Now my brother and I don't have to worry about making any wrong decisions. Mom and Dad have told us everything we need to know.

The Civil War Gun

Over the years, many people have called me or approached me after a speech to ask about the proper approach to distributing heirlooms. Interestingly enough, the *things* seemed to weigh more on their minds than their parents' estate plans. Heirlooms are an important part of any estate plan, including their values, but they are secondary to nurturing family relationships. Let me tell you a story you can probably relate to. If this hasn't happened to you, it has happened to someone you know.

I was speaking to a group of seniors, encouraging them to distribute heirlooms to their children prior to death to avoid or at least minimize the possibility of feuding, when I was interrupted by an elderly gentleman who stood up and announced, "I have a problem, Ms. Hall."

"What can I help you with?" I asked.

"Well, you see, I have two sons and only one Civil War firearm that has been passed down for generations. They are already fighting over it, and I'm not even dead yet. What should I do? I'm really torn up over this."

Realizing where this was going, I gently asked, "What would *you* like to do about it?"

After a moment of thought, he said he would like his older son to have it but was afraid the younger one would be very upset with him. What he said next made the hair on the back of my neck stand up. "*I think I will just let them fight over it after I'm gone!*" What was even more unnerving was that the audience broke out in laughter at this remark. But I was the one holding the microphone, so I decided to get everyone's attention and use this moment as a teaching tool.

"Excuse me," I said loudly into the microphone. The laughter began to die down. "Sir, you don't want to let your sons fight it out, and let me explain why so everyone in this room will understand that that is the worst thing you could ever do." The room fell silent.

"I can see you are in quite a pickle with this decision, but the decision ultimately belongs to *you*. The responsibility falls on you, the father, just like it did when your sons were growing up and you taught them right from wrong. Sometimes you had to get tough with them to teach them the lesson at hand. The same is true when passing down and dividing heirlooms.

"Here's what you should do: have the firearm professionally appraised, and then call a meeting with both of your boys only. No grandchildren, no wives, just you and your two sons at your home, so you are on your territory [this gentleman was a widower; otherwise, I would have included his wife]. Tell them you do not want any fighting now or at the time of your death regarding this firearm; therefore, you have made some decisions while you are alive and have a say-so. Your plans are for the elder son to take possession of the firearm *today*. It is okay to tell your sons that you had trouble with this decision, but make sure they understand this is what you want. Then hand the younger son a check for the exact amount the gun was appraised, and let him take any other asset in the home. Even if the younger son does get a little upset over this, at least he won't fight with his brother anymore because you have spoken."

Your parents may be older now, but if they are capable, they can still call the shots with their children. And they should because left to their own accord, a majority of the time, the children will not divide the estate peacefully.

When a parent dies, the family glue has a tendency to weaken, at least for a while and sometimes for decades if bad decisions are made. If parents call the shots prior to their deaths or at least have their wishes fully documented for each child, there will be less fighting among the surviving family members. It may not stop the arguing, but it will diminish it because children will often still respect their parents' wishes even after they are gone (not always but most of the time).

Note to Parents

The key to keeping things fair is *to be honest and equal at all times to all children* unless you have reasons otherwise, and tell your children about your wishes now. Talk with all your children at the same time, if possible, and make sure all your children are included in all correspondence detailing your wishes about your estate. If you just let your children fight it out at the time of your death, the entire family will be dragged through the wreckage, and I can make you one guarantee: your children won't just resent each other for the week of your funeral; they will resent each other for the remainder of their lives, probably wishing you had made the decision for them. Since you didn't make the decision, they will also resent *you* for the rest of their lives, which is not the legacy you'd want to leave.

Which brings us right back to my advice. If you love your kids, and I know you do, *do not do this to them*. Part of being a good parent is making difficult decisions regarding your death and what happens after your death. No one likes to face this, but it is a part of life. Wouldn't you rather leave this earth with peace of mind? Someday, your kids will thank you and not resent you. Now that's a legacy I could live with!

Care for One Another

Ideally, you will begin to talk with your siblings about the future before your parents enter a health crisis, but you may not have that luxury. For example, your dad may be in great health but fall and become incapacitated. Or your parents may be in an automobile accident, and suddenly you are in crisis mode. If this happens, your first priority is to provide comfort for one another and your families, but even then you can gently broach the subject: "Sis, I know we're both really hurting from this, but let's try to get together, just you and me, and figure out what to do next." Don't try to resolve everything then and there, but simply open the door to meet and talk about next steps. The more compassion you show toward your siblings, the more receptive everyone will be to addressing the issues related to your parents' estate.

If you have more than one sibling, agree that you will never meet unless everyone is present. Even if one of your siblings lives far away and gives you permission to meet without him, don't do it. If a face-to-face meeting is impossible, get the absent sibling on a speakerphone so at least everyone hears what the other is saying. I've found that in the emotional upheaval following a parent's death, people often mask their feelings, only later to accuse the others of making important decisions behind their backs. By the way, I've said it before, but these meetings should not include spouses. I know some will disagree with me here, but in my experience it's usually an in-law who fuels the fight over property. Just be consistent, and stay out of the fray when your spouse faces a similar loss.

An Ounce of Prevention

Family discord will be minimized if you employ the following strategies:

- Make sure your parents have prepared a will and a wish list.
- Understand your attitude as well as your siblings' when it comes to your parents' possessions.

- Talk about the future with your parents.

- Communicate openly and regularly with your siblings.

- Honor your parents' wishes over your own.

- Settle disputes creatively rather than legally.

Be Creative

I'd like to leave you with one final strategy for keeping the peace with your siblings when tensions rise over a particular item that you all want and that wasn't covered by the will. Try to settle your differences creatively rather than legally.

One really outlandish settlement option is something you learned in kindergarten, and it's called sharing. Suppose your dad was an avid fisherman and owned the ideal fishing boat—one of those slick bass boats with a powerful outboard, a tackle box full of lures, and several fishing poles. For whatever reason—either there was no will or he didn't update it after he bought the boat—there's no clear instruction for who inherits the boat. You and your siblings can fight over it for years while it sits unused, or you can share it. For example, Jim gets it one summer; Bill the next. Or Jim keeps it at his place, but Bill can use it for a weekend when Jim isn't fishing. Or here's a novel idea: Jim and Bill become fishing buddies and use it together. Sometimes we make things way too complicated when a little creative thinking is all that's needed to keep everyone happy.

I've known families who circulated a favorite vase or figurine between themselves, and each time they passed it along to the next sibling, it became an opportunity to reminisce about their parents. Other creative solutions include donating a valuable yet disputed piece to a museum or nonprofit organization where it can be displayed permanently in honor of your parents. Draw straws or flip a coin and let the "loser" select two items as compensation. Another option would be to sell the piece outright and divide the proceeds equally among heirs.

A Wolf in Sheep's Clothing

Most of the disputes you may experience as you attempt to fairly divide your parents' property can be successfully resolved or even prevented by following the advice I've outlined in "An Ounce of Prevention." However, sometimes things will get out of control, and you may need to take action quickly to prevent a sibling or family friend from taking advantage.

A few years ago, I was called by a middle-aged woman who had been legally designated as executrix of her parents' estate. Although she did her best to divide the contents of the home equally among herself and two brothers, she noticed that many important pieces of jewelry were slowly disappearing. She would be in one room with one of her brothers, and a sister-in-law would be going through the jewelry box, taking what she wanted. Even when I arrived on the scene to bring a little order to the process, one of the brothers picked up a beautiful antique diamond necklace and simply declared he would be taking it.

"Okay, if you want that piece, you can have it, as long as the other two siblings do not want it," I told him. "But it's worth twenty-five thousand dollars, so you won't be taking anything else until your brother and sister have also each taken twenty-five thousand dollars' worth of your parents' property."

He glared at me and replied, "What? You don't really mean that, do you?"

"Absolutely," I countered, as he sheepishly put the diamond necklace back in the jewelry box. He knew I had called his bluff.

After that, with me at the helm to mediate, no one in that family got the lion's share. Financial equality is 100 percent necessary to divide an estate appropriately. This is why you must know the worth of these possessions before the division process begins.

Blended Family Battles

Everything I have written so far assumed that you are part of what is called a traditional family. That is, your parents have remained married to each other, or you have at least one sibling. But I realize that divorce crept into some of the marriages of our parents' generation, and you may be facing some unique situations as you deal with the loss of your final parent. If this describes your situation, I know I don't need to tell you that the blessings of a blended family as a result of divorce or the death of a parent also bring with them some awkward and uncomfortable issues.

For example, if you have a stepbrother or stepsister from a second marriage, should either be included in the distribution of heirlooms or wealth? Will the second spouse receive the bulk of the estate over the blood children? All of this depends on the clarity of the will and estate planning between the parents and stepparents.

In general terms, you treat the distribution of property the same way you would if your family was not blended. Try to get your parents to make these decisions early and not leave it up to you and your siblings to figure out. Make sure your parents update their will when they remarry. Stay close to your siblings, blended or otherwise. In other words, prepare as much as you can ahead of time. But you still may need to make a tough call.

Wills are of vast importance in all scenarios, but blended family situations can turn ugly, especially if there is no will. I strongly encourage you to speak with an estate planning attorney to get all the specifics about blended families. I remember the time a client remarried after being widowed. He died shortly after they got married and did not have a will. In his state, the new wife got half of his estate, and his blood children got the other half. The children were not happy! This is why planning is so important.

I write an advice column for a newspaper, and recently one of the subscribers sent in this question: "Several years ago I was divorced, and shortly after I met and married a wonderful divorcée. My wife and I are now in retirement and beginning to think about how we want to divide our property after we are gone. The problem is, our blended family is already fighting over one particular heirloom, and we don't know what to do about it. Any suggestions?"

More than 40 percent of my clients come from some type of blended-family situation, so I tried to think back on what some of these clients did. The first thing I did in my column was remind them that they are the parents. Regardless of how old your children are, you are the parent, and *you* decide what to do with your property. Then I recommended that any heirloom that was a part of the first marriage should go only to the children from that marriage. This applies both ways, for in this case, the man's wife was previously married, so my advice was that anything from her side of the family should go to her biological children. This, at least, will keep it simple. Distribution of these items should take place while the parents are still living to avoid future feuding among stepchildren. I could write volumes on that topic!

What If You Are an Only Child?

If you're an only child, there's good news and bad. On the good side, you don't have anyone to fight with. The downside is that you have to go it alone and won't have anyone to help you. Since you are in the midst of this task alone, or so it feels, remember, there are many who would be more than willing to assist you.

If you have cousins, they may be willing to lend a helping hand, or perhaps an aunt or uncle can make some phone calls on your behalf. Local churches usually have teams of volunteers to help those with all sorts of challenges, and high schools and colleges often have a place on campus you can go to or call to hire students for a day or weekend. Remember, too, that there are professionals in this industry who can help you through this process. Think of this process as if you are a manager, and now you need to learn how to delegate.

I remember Holly well. At forty-nine, she was married with three children when her mother and father unexpectedly passed away within four months of each other. Needless to say, Holly was devastated. Not only were her emotions at an all-time high, but she was left with a home filled with stuff from her parents and grandparents in a town several states away from her home. As an only child, she had so many questions: "Where do I begin? How do I get rid of everything in this house? How do I sort through all of their paperwork? How do I know what things are worth? I can't possibly do this by myself!"

This type of stress can take on many forms, including anxiety and panic, digestive disturbances, and migraines. However, halting these physical inconveniences is paramount, and the way to do that is enlist some help. Put together an army of your own, and begin to master the art of delegation. Holly was very smart. She called and visited many of the neighbors who were close friends of her parents. They seemed to understand her challenge of being an only child, and they selected two weekends to pitch in and help Holly clean out the garage, attic, and closets. Holly hired an appraiser to determine the items of value in her parents' home. Only then could she make clear decisions on what should be sold and how it should be sold.

The friends and neighbors who came together to help Holly with her challenge also offered her support in many ways during the process. Holly even reconnected with a couple of childhood friends. She was fortunate in that none of these friends and neighbors were *takers*, and each had a genuine interest in assisting her. By the end of those two weekends, her parents' house had become cleared out, utilizing my suggestions in chapter 11. What was left over was very manageable for her to make a few last remaining decisions.

As I am often found saying, "You are never alone." If you look, you will find caring people to help you, but you must ask for help. Holly's story ended up being a happy ending, and yours can too.

I know there's no such thing as a perfect family, and we usually discover that in times of crisis and loss. You can prevent your imperfections and those of your siblings from dividing your family by preparing for the eventual loss of your parents. Take stock of your own character traits as well as those of your siblings, and do your best to not be the greedy relative or any of the other less desirable relatives I characterized earlier. Talk about the future with your parents and siblings while your mom and dad are still healthy. Keep your conversation positive and compassionate. Honor your parents' wishes over your own, and when tempted to fight over an object, consider sharing it instead. After all, you're a family.

What Do I Do Now?

Current situation: you are beginning the process of cleaning out your parents' estate.

☑ *Call a "siblings only" meeting.* When a parent dies, ask your siblings to meet with you and the surviving parent or just with you if this was your last surviving parent. Discuss plans for the funeral and any other matters that need to be taken care of. Spouses should stay in the background until invited in. No offense meant. Just keep it simple, and kindly keep spouses out of it.

☑ *Guard the key.* Make sure the executor of the will has a key to the home. Other siblings may be given access to the home, but just to be safe, the executor should be present whenever anyone visits the home.

☑ *Ask for help.* If you are an only child, ask for help with the many challenges that come with clearing out the house. If you are part of a blended family, ask your siblings to work together regarding assets so the blended family will not feud.

Seven

Scammers, Schemers, and Other Scoundrels

Part of the burden facing boomers is trying to protect their parents from unscrupulous people who prey on the elderly. Sadly, the most prevalent predators are people who are familiar with the family. Until you experience this, you will probably think I'm exaggerating, but I'm not. I see it all the time, as I did in Laura's case.

I never met Laura, but I am told she was one of the kindest, most generous people you could ever know. She had died at the age of sixty-two after a long battle with cancer and left the executrix, a close female friend, quite a mess. Laura, a divorcée, was a retired secretary and lived in a modest three-bedroom home filled to the hilt with stuff—good stuff, bad stuff, and "What *is* this?" kind of stuff. Upon a quick Estate Lady evaluation, it all began to look alike. Laura apparently had been addicted to home shopping channels and bought almost everything in sight.

Many, many boxes that had been delivered to her home were left untouched by the front door. Her jewelry boxes were overflowing with all kinds of shopping network rings, bracelets, earrings, and necklaces. Every imaginable gadget and home-improvement gizmo were scattered all over the home. It just didn't make sense because Laura lived alone and had no children and no companion. Why would she possibly order all of these things?

The executrix knew that for a long time, Laura had suffered from depression, and buying all of these things brought her comfort. There are many types of addiction, but obsessive-compulsive buying didn't seem to be that dreadful until the executrix discovered Laura was more than $200,000 in debt, and her estate was only worth $140,000. Laura died knowing the mess she was leaving behind and did not share it with anyone, probably for fear of being scrutinized and abandoned in her final days.

The estate contents had to be sold in an orderly liquidation sooner rather than later to pay off some of the debt. The executrix was in a hornet's nest, and handling this estate took her away from her own life for the better part of a year.

Here's the most difficult part of the story. One day while we were there setting up for the estate sale, the executrix dropped in to let us know that two of Laura's friends were coming by to select clothes for themselves, and the remainder of the clothing they would take to a mission. My antenna (and multiple red flags) flew up instantly! I cautioned the executrix, "Let's think about this for a moment. The jewelry is in the closet where all the clothes are. We have taken inventory but haven't brought it out yet to price. There is so much of it to go through. Maybe I should go put the jewelry in a safe place."

The executrix told me that the person coming over was one of Laura's best friends and to have no worries. Besides, the best friend had already taken several good pieces of jewelry ahead of time and got what she wanted because she was supposed to get cash assets, but since there was no cash . . . she got a few jewelry pieces. The plot thickens.

My antenna was still sticking straight up! You don't do this kind of work for this long and not have excellent gut instinct. "I still don't feel good about this," I repeated. "Would you please consider staying to watch them while we are handling matters on the other side of the house?" I would at least feel better knowing the executrix was with the friends while we were busy setting up for the estate sale, unable to watch them. So the executrix stayed but not in the room where the closet was because she "felt funny about it" as though she was spying on Laura's best friend. She didn't feel comfortable, so she went out in the yard, in the garage, anywhere *but* the bedroom closet where the jewelry was.

We knew the exact boxes all the jewelry pieces were in because we had done an inventory. I distinctly remember a huge sapphire ring, gold brace-lets, and a smoky topaz bracelet in one trinket box. Well, Laura's friends were in that closet for two hours and didn't take one article of clothing, not for themselves and not even for the mission. All of Laura's clothes remained hanging exactly the same as before they arrived. It was obvious that their real mission was to go in there and steal from Laura. And steal they did. As soon as they left, I headed for that closet and instantly spotted many pieces that had been there that morning prior to their arrival were now gone. I sat in the closet, not knowing what to tell the executrix. It wasn't as if I could approach her and say, "I tried to tell you, but you didn't heed my advice." I had to find the right words to break it to her gently.

Several thousand dollars' worth of jewelry went missing from Laura's estate, and that was money that could have been applied to her debt. My guess is that the best friend took that jewelry because she felt cheated out of her inheritance and thus "entitled" to take it.

The executrix was extremely distraught when I told her that the pieces were missing. She was understandably angry with the friend but decided not to confront her; she had been through enough and did not want to cause any more waves. Then she offered me another tidbit to this story. Prior to her passing, Laura had accused the best friend of staeling from her. Laura had apparently caught her friend, who had been in the closet while laura had been asleep. But no one believed Laura; they thought the medication ws talking. Now I ask you, what's worse: stealing from a friend or stealing from a deceased friend? Sometimes, there just aren't enough words to describe the horror of what I see.

When it comes to your parents' valuables, you need to be watchful and wise. It is not mean-spirited to simply keep an eye on anyone who wants to visit the home after your parents are deceased. It's just good common sense. Even when you take precautions to protect your parents' valuables, bad things can still happen as I learned with "the diamond lady."

The Diamond Lady

Frances, a wealthy woman in the advanced stages of a terminal illness, was blind, hearing impaired, and afflicted with severe memory impairment. In short, she no longer recognized any family members or anyone else. She had never married and had no children, but she did have four beneficiaries to her estate, and all four really loved her and provided for her the very best care in a beautiful facility for the remainder of her days.

One of Frances's passions in life was purchasing fine diamonds, and she had several pieces that were very large and easily valued in the six-figure range. Every day she wore them because she loved them. Frances was bathed in them, napped in them, slept in them, ate in them, and so on.

The beneficiaries started to grow concerned about these pieces (among other assets) for a number of very logical reasons. Most people don't own pieces as valuable as these, and if they did, they might be kept in a place such as a safe, vault, or bank safe-deposit box. So the beneficiaries did the right thing in requesting that the earrings and bracelets be removed while Frances was napping and to have the genuine diamonds replaced with other, less expensive stones. The genuine diamonds would then be turned over to the trustee of the estate. The beneficiaries were promised these diamonds, a generous gift as well as investment pieces, upon Frances's death. Who could possibly blame them for wanting them protected?

Unfortunately, the diamond pieces disappeared one day prior to their request being fulfilled. Not only did the large diamond pieces worth approximately $180,000 disappear, but a video camera, some CDs, and a Crock-Pot vanished as well from Frances's place. This was a clear indication that the caregiver or someone who had very close contact with Frances had made off with the goods. The beneficiaries were beside themselves. How could this happen? Why didn't anyone prevent this from happening? Why didn't anyone listen to their request? But with all the questions and accusations that flew, the damage had been done. The diamonds were long gone, never to be found again, probably sold at a pawn shop for a few thousand dollars.

That being said, it is important for me to state that I think the world of caregivers. I call many of them earth angels because that is what they are. But as in any occupation in the world, there are good and not-so-good caregivers out there.

It is up to us to make the correct decisions to care for and protect our loved ones who cannot make decisions for themselves or about their assets. For the record, I think this story clearly demonstrates that we must exercise extreme caution with valuables. Remember to have valuable items evaluated by a professional, have those values documented, and keep the items in a safe place until they are distributed to family or sold. The faces of exploitation are often familiar faces and not necessarily strangers.

The Unprofessional Professional

Sometimes the scammers are the professionals you hire to help you with your parents' estate. In my experience, I have found that working with another professional can be a rewarding experience because we can utilize each other's strengths and assistance. And so, we will from time to time, turn to each other for help.

I had consulted with a colleague to help me sell a couple of estate items for which I was confident she had solid buyers. I signed a contract with that person to sell these pieces on behalf of one of my clients and agreed to split the commission with her. The first piece sold quickly, and payment was received promptly. The second, more valuable piece, however, appeared to have dropped off the face of the earth.

Suddenly, all communication with my colleague ceased. This person would not return phone calls, e-mails, or letters. I got the Better Business Bureau involved, but there still was no response from my colleague. I hired an attorney, who suggested it would cost three times the value of the piece to hire him. It's not as if I didn't have a specific, legally binding contract with this person. According to my attorney, this kind of unscrupulous individual *knows* she can get away with it, which is why she did it. I did the only thing I could do and wrote a check to my client for the fair market value of that piece. To this day, that experience has crawled under my skin and remains there, irritating me every time I think of the ordeal. I never did hear back from that unprofessional professional.

Here's the urgent message I would like you to take from this distasteful experience: if a colleague is willing to take advantage of me, a professional with years of experience, what is that person going to do to you, especially in the midst of crisis? I think this is worth some serious thought. So that you may have further peace of mind in this kind of situation, please refer to chapter 10 for practical guidance on how to hire the right professional.

Dealing with Dealers

Some dealers have been known to offer lowball values on items in the home. For example, they will say to the boomer or older parent, "I'll give you twenty-three hundred dollars for everything in the house, but that offer is good for today only." Or they might say, "Take it or leave it" because they know you are overwhelmed and do not want to deal with all of the stuff.

In situations like these, I suggest that it might be prudent to leave it. In these homes, where I have been and heard these stories from wise clients who said no to these people, I have found items worth thousands of dollars that the dealer offered very little on. On the other hand, if there are no valuables in the home and you are certain this person is doing you a true favor, use that dealer, and harness his strength to help you clear out the home—but be certain first.

As in other occupations, you will find good dealers and not-so-good dealers. Dealers want to make a profit, and we are all in business to do so, but finding a dealer that is fair is the hard part. By occupation I am a liquidator, which means I will get closer to wholesale than retail, but my clients are aware of this going in; everything is explained to them in detail. When items of significant value are found, all efforts are made to broker the piece at the highest possible price by finding the right buyer, making my clients quite content when that happens. But if an antique table is worth $1,500, many will come in and offer $200. If you empower yourself by knowing the worth of those items first, no one can exploit you.

Cash Paid for Collectibles

If you see someone advertising "Cash Paid for Collectibles," these ads can be very alluring, especially if you have things lying around the attic, garage, barn, or basement. After all, you probably prefer cash for these items you no longer want or need, and I don't blame you. Often I will find ads from collectors searching for items to add to their personal collections, like military items, toy trains, antique dolls, and so on. Having been a collector twenty years ago, I was willing to pay top dollar for what I was looking for, and my guess is that many collectors out there are genuine and feel the same way. However, some might be looking to acquire items to resell. Again, I caution you to know what you have first, and *then* sell it for a fair price. A die-hard collector will truly cherish these items and generally offer more for them.

The Heir Who Felt Entitled to Everything

At first glance he seemed like a nice guy, filled with sorrow at the loss of his beloved grandmother. It should be known immediately in this story that no will could be found. The grandmother's estate was now in the hands of a law firm, and I had been consulted to evaluate and then sell the contents of her home.

The grandson, upon hearing the news that everything was to be sold and the cash proceeds to be divided among all heirs, became irrational and out of control. "My grandmother wanted me to have everything! I was her favorite! I'm supposed to get it all! This is not the way it is supposed to happen!" It was hard to watch because, as explained in chapter 3, when someone dies without a will, the state decides how the assets are distributed, not the grandson or any other family member. In this case, I was called in to sell it all.

The attorney's office made it clear that I could not distribute anything to anyone in the family. Personal items, such as photo frames, were to be sold, not given to the heirs. Each day I was in the home preparing for the estate sale, the grandson would beat on the doors and harass me for doing my job. "Let me in or else! That's my stuff! You'd better let me in!"

The attorney's office decided to change all locks on the house for fear that items would disappear if the grandson gained entrance. When the grandson realized he could not get in through me and discovered new locks were installed, he started sending over his friends to threaten me.

Through it all, the attorney never wavered, and neither did I. We finally told the grandson that if he wanted anything special, he was welcome to come to the estate sale and purchase any of the items he wanted. He was angry at this, too, because he said everything rightfully belonged to him and no one else. Interestingly enough, the law firm had discovered there were twelve living heirs to the estate, and that meant it had to be divided twelve ways. This, of course, sent the grandson over the edge, so I hired a police officer to be at the estate sale to protect me and the contents. The estate sale went very well, and he did purchase multiple items from the estate.

In the long run, we discovered two very interesting facts about this grandson. First, he was already wealthy and could have purchased all the estate contents if he so desired. Second, evidence was later discovered that he had found his grandmother's will and destroyed it, thinking all her assets would go to him because he was Grandma's favorite.

It didn't exactly work out the way this schemer wanted it to, did it? Personally, I had always wondered if he loved his grandma so much, why he never called her, visited her, had anyone vacuum her home (which had not been cleaned in years), or cleared her cupboards of outdated food.

Identity Theft Isn't Just for the Living

In estates, I find that a lot of the boomers attempt to clean out their moms and dads' homes, only to give up after a valiant effort. We find many personal financial papers, tax returns, investment portfolios, and so on in the trash without benefit of being shredded or destroyed. I cannot stress to you enough the importance of calling shredding companies and having them come to the house to do the shredding right in the driveway. It is an added expense but one certainly worthwhile. These days we can't be too careful.

If your parents are still living and you want to assist them in protecting their assets, you had better make sure someone isn't fast-talking them into poverty. According to those who investigate these crimes against our Greatest Generation, people over the age of sixty-five constitute anywhere from 30 to 50 percent of all fraud victims.

It's bad enough that these vultures prey on people who should be enjoying their golden years, but the schemes continue even after they die. I learned of one couple who were talked into paying for a prefuneral package that was supposed to handle all the funeral and burial costs when they died. Yet by the time they died, the company had gone out of business, and the family had to pay for their father's funeral out of their own pockets.

Fast Facts

- 50 percent of elderly Americans are victims of financial exploitation.
- 70 percent of the nation's net worth is owned by those fifty or older.
- As many as five million seniors are victims of financial exploitation annually.
- The fastest-growing segment of the population described as elderly are those over eighty-five.
- The average age of a victim of financial exploitation is seventy-eight.[1]

Why Your Parents Are Vulnerable

When adult children learn that their parents have been conned, they are sometimes surprised and often angry. "Dad is a pretty sharp guy when it comes to money. How in the world did he fall for that scheme?" We've often gone to our parents for financial advice, so the last thing we usually worry about as our parents age is their vulnerability to these kinds of fraudulent pitches. Why would our intelligent parents, who are generally known for their frugality, convert a safe mutual fund into a high-risk investment that could potentially drain their retirement fund?

First, seniors tend to be trusting. They realize that times change and often feel they have not kept up with those changes. So when a friendly voice calls and offers to help them earn more money on a newfangled investment, they listen. Couple that with the fact that many seniors live alone, have little contact with people, and love it when someone takes an interest in them. These telemarketers know that and often begin their calls conversationally with questions about the senior's family, her health, whether or not she has a pet, and the pet's name. Imagine your mom, all by herself, and she gets a call from a cheery young man who really cares about her life. Do you think she's going to hang up the phone? Of course not! By the time the caller gets around to his pitch, he seems like a friend, certainly not someone who would try to cheat her.

Second, seniors are also vulnerable to these schemes because they tend to worry about their financial security. Many are watching their nest eggs dwindle as they dip into savings to pay for expensive prescription medicine and other health care costs. And they know that one day they may have to move into some form of assisted living and wonder how they are going to pay for it. So any promise of quick returns on an investment catches their attention.

Scammers also know another important fact about most seniors: they have money and valuable possessions. These con artists will try anything to pry that money away from unsuspecting seniors. One of their favorite tactics is to appeal to the generosity and altruistic intentions of the senior. While a great many charities are honest, ethical enterprises that ease the pain and suffering of less fortunate people, an occasional rotten apple creates a sham nonprofit, develops a slick brochure or telephone appeal, and bilks caring seniors out of millions. Sadly, watchdog agencies who monitor charities report that human tragedies, such as 9/11, the tsunami in Asia, Hurricane Katrina, and even the tragic shootings at Virginia Tech and Northern Illinois University, always bring out fraudulent charities who prey on the unsuspecting.

How to Help Protect Your Parents

When someone takes advantage of your parents, they are also stealing from you. I have seen too many occasions when a parent dies, and as the family goes through the financial records, they discover the once-substantial savings account has nearly disappeared. So it's a double tragedy that you can help prevent by learning how dishonest people try to cheat the elderly and by keeping a watchful eye on your parents.

One of the first things you can do to protect your parents from scammers and cheaters is to recognize the signs that often accompany such abuse. Keep in mind, however, that if a senior has been exploited, he is usually too embarrassed to admit it. In fact, although approximately 50 percent of elderly Americans are victims of financial exploitation, only 10 to 15 percent of such abuse is reported.[2] That, coupled with the fact that your parents may be closemouthed about their finances, makes it difficult to know if anything improper is going on.

The following may indicate that your parents are being victimized:

- Sudden bank account changes, especially an unexplained withdrawal of large sums of money
- Unfamiliar names listed as signatories on a bank signature card
- Unfamiliar long-distance telephone numbers, especially from overseas, on their monthly bill
- Significantly lower standard of living (change in eating and shopping habits; unable to afford things they once afforded)
- Selling higher-end items such as furniture, antiques, and so on
- Sudden disappearance of valuable possessions
- Increase in commercial or junk mail
- Sudden changes in behavior; symptoms of depression or anxiety
- Increased worries over money

In order to recognize most of these warning signs, someone in the family needs to have access to otherwise private, personal information. That is why I recommend in chapter 3 that a family member be given power of attorney for both parents. Not only will that expedite the execution of the estate after your parents die, but it provides the necessary safeguards to protect them while they are living. Many parents, especially widowed, elderly women, appreciate help in paying their monthly bills and managing their financial accounts. Try to understand their natural suspicion of anyone going through their financial records—how would you like it if one of your kids went through your mail?—and approach them accordingly. If they know you are trying to help them instead of just being nosy, they are more likely to consent.

Six Ways to Protect Your Parents from Fraud

1. Ask or discuss with your parents who has durable power of attorney.

2. Register your parents' telephone number(s) with the National Do Not Call Registry (www.donotcall.gov).

3. Discuss with them the list of common frauds (outlined in this chapter) and ask them to contact you if they suspect anyone is trying to defraud them.

4. Ask your parents to contact you if anyone offers to buy any of their possessions.

5. Make sure a family member personally visits your parents on a weekly basis. If this is a challenge and you have other siblings, take turns.

6. Reduce junk mail for a small fee by going to either of these Web sites: www.stopthejunkmail.com and www.greendimes.com.

Common Frauds Against Senior Citizens

The U.S. Securities and Exchange Commission is the government agency responsible for making sure any business engaged in investing money for other people operates ethically. On September 7, 2007, the chairman of the commission, Christopher Cox, testified before the United States Senate Special Committee on Aging. The topic of the day: financial fraud against the elderly. A very bright and capable leader, Cox presented convincing evidence that while scam artists hit people of all ages, the elderly are particularly vulnerable. He reported on how his commission worked with the Riverside County

(California) district attorney to shut down a scheme that bilked seniors out of a total of $144.8 million. He explained how another outfit preyed on seniors by offering them a free lunch, and then pressured them to invest in high-risk investments. By the time his office got involved, most of the money invested was already lost.[3]

But what really got my attention is how scammers preyed on Cox's own parents. His father was unable to make sound decisions due to Alzheimer's, and his mother could barely speak because of throat cancer. Unscrupulous brokers pestered her repeatedly over the phone and in person to convert her safe, low-interest home mortgage into a short-term loan with a huge balloon payment. Even though Cox personally intervened and ordered these con artists to quit bothering his parents, they persisted. Had she fallen for their sales pitch, she would have lost her home when the balloon payment came due.

In addition to scams that are directly related to your parents' estate, seniors are also vulnerable to some general frauds that *indirectly* relate to their estate in that they can deplete their wealth and thus leave little behind. Here are some of the most common scams against the elderly and ways you can protect your parents from them:

Home-repair fraud. A truck pulls into the driveway of your parents' home, and a gentleman approaches your mom and claims he has just finished sealing a neighbor's driveway and has leftover sealant. He quotes a very reasonable price, and your mom can't pass up a bargain. A few hours later, when the job is finished, the gentleman hands your mom a bill for three times the amount he quoted. She protests mildly, but the man insists he had to use more sealant than he thought, and he needs to be paid. He even offers to drive her to the bank if she needs to withdraw money to pay him. She's a little intimidated and writes him a check. Senior scammers use this same approach for roofing jobs and gutter repair.

Warn your parents against authorizing any type of home repair until they check out references and get a written estimate. They should never agree to anything on the spot; instead, they should ask for a day or two to think it over. Ask your parents to always call you before they agree to any home repair.

Utility employee impersonators. Two people show up and claim they are from the utility company and that they have come to correct an overcharge on their bill. One of them produces a hundred-dollar bill to repay the overcharge of a lesser amount. As the senior makes change, they note where she keeps her money. Then one "employee" diverts the senior by having her join him in the basement to check for gas leaks while the other steals cash or valuables.

Tell your parents to never let anyone inside their house without asking to see identification. If the visitor produces identification, your parents should ask him to wait while they call the company. If the employee is legitimate, he'll wait. If not, he'll be gone in a flash.

The pigeon drop. This is one of the oldest scams around, showing up year after year in towns and cities across America. A stranger approaches a senior, claiming to have found a large bag containing cash. The senior is convinced to put up *good faith* money to share in the find and is driven to his bank to obtain the money. The good faith money is put in another bag, and while the victim is distracted, the bags are switched. The stranger leaves to make final arrangements, and the senior is literally left holding the bag . . . of wadded-up paper. Naturally, the stranger disappears with the victim's money.

You would think the if-it's-too-good-to-be-true warning would prevent this common scam from occurring, but it keeps happening. Tell your parents what they told you when you were a child: never talk to strangers. Also, tell them never to withdraw money from a bank at a stranger's request. And if anyone approaches them with a story of a found bag of money, they should excuse themselves and call the police.

Bank examiner scam. Similar to the pigeon drop, the con artist approaches a senior, posing as a bank official, police officer, or FBI agent. He usually flashes an official-looking badge or other identification and requests the senior's help in checking on an employee suspected of defrauding the senior's bank. He then asks the victim to withdraw cash from his account, assuring him the money will be returned after the investigation is complete. Of course, the "official" disappears, and the money is gone forever.

Again, tell your parents to never withdraw money at the request of anyone. Banks never operate this way.

Ponzi schemes and other investment rip-offs. Someone, often a friend or acquaintance of the family, approaches your parents with a promise of huge returns if they invest in this person's new business. The payoff is usually promised quickly, as in "You will double your investment in thirty days." And many times, the promise is delivered, so your parents may enthusiastically refer their friends to this amazing investment opportunity. So far, so good. Who wouldn't want their parents to expand their nest egg so quickly?

But behind the scenes, this investment superstar is robbing Peter to pay Paul—he uses the money he got from other unsuspecting investors to pay off your parents. But he has to keep finding new investors to pay off the next victim. Everyone indeed gets their money—until he runs out of new investors. Then, someone who hasn't gotten his return alerts the authorities, and this house of cards comes crashing down. So what happens to all the money your parents earned? Usually the courts step in, demands that everyone relinquish their profits plus the original investment, and then things get divided up. Your parents will be lucky to retrieve a tenth of their original investment. For some reason, Ponzi schemes seem to be more prevalent among churchgoing people.

Remind your parents to be wary of anything that sounds too good to be true. If they are even slightly tempted to take their hard-earned money out of a safe account, ask them to meet with a financial planner to discuss the opportunity.

Fraudulent charities. Whenever there is a national or international disaster, scammers come out of the woodwork. Usually, these are people who go door-to-door, asking for small cash donations. Seniors are especially vulnerable to them because of their generosity and desire to help those in need. Plus, these counterfeit solicitors only ask for a few dollars. While the potential for loss is not great, people on fixed incomes who drop a twenty-dollar bill in a bucket may not be able to buy their medicine that month.

Warn your parents against any door-to-door solicitation. Most reputable charities have abandoned that once-common practice precisely because it encourages fraud. If your parents indicate their desire to contribute to victims of a major tragedy, refer them to national organizations such as the American

Red Cross, United Way, or World Vision. You should also encourage them to inquire at their local church or synagogue about relief efforts these religious institutions sponsor.

These types of scams target your parents' money. They may seem unbelievable, and you may think your parents are too smart to fall for them, but every year thousands of seniors get ripped off by these schemes. Your efforts to educate your parents will significantly reduce the chances of their falling for these frauds.

National Center for Elder Abuse

The National Center for Elder Abuse is an excellent resource for information on financial and other forms of abuse against senior citizens. It publishes reports and conducts research on this growing problem. NCEA's mission is to promote understanding, knowledge sharing, and action on elder abuse, neglect, and exploitation. Its Web site also offers links to other excellent resources and organizations also devoted to protecting senior citizens. You may contact the NCEA at:

National Center on Elder Abuse, National Association of State Units on Aging
1201 15th Street NW, Suite 350
Washington, DC 20005

Phone: (202) 898-2586
E-mail: NCEA@nasua.org
Web site: www.elderabusecenter.org

Trading Places

When you were a child, your parents did their best to protect you from all sorts of dangers that kids face. They taught you to look both ways before you crossed the street, never talk to strangers, wash your hands before you eat, and always wear clean underwear in case you get in an accident. If you're a guy, your dad probably taught you gun safety; if you're a woman, your mom probably taught you how to watch out for certain boys. They did this because they loved you and didn't want anything bad to happen to you. One of the strange and somewhat sad realities of life is that point where our parents can no longer protect us and, in fact, need us to protect them.

Because it seems so unnatural to parent our parents, many of us take the head-in-the-sand approach and hope nothing too serious happens to our moms and dads. But eventually the situation becomes inevitable. I hope this chapter has alerted you to some of the despicable practices people use to prey on older people. It is time to step up to the plate and protect your parents. Think of how hard your mom and dad have worked to enjoy their home and possessions and have enough money set aside to help them live comfortably during these golden years. They want nothing more than to be able to share that with you after they're gone, but they are vulnerable, as all of us can be. One of the worst parts of my job is to inform aging parents that they have been victimized by fraud. Almost always, they are not sad for themselves but express such regret that the things they hoped to leave for their children are gone.

Honor your parents by standing between them and anything or anyone who sees them as an easy target.

What Do I Do Now?

Current situation: your parents live by themselves and are showing signs of becoming more infirm.

☑ *Warn your parents.* Explain to your parents every scam outlined in this chapter.

☑ *Monitor your parents' finances.* If your parents give you permission, regularly check their bank accounts to identify any unusual transactions.

☑ *Review offers.* Call your parents and ask them to contact you anytime they receive a special offer in the mail, on the telephone, over radio or television, or in person.

Eight

The Nitty-Gritty of Dividing Your Parents' Estate

The Stewarts were lovely people. It was obvious to me they raised four children to really love their parents and one another. Mom and Dad Stewart had made some difficult decisions prior to becoming infirm. Mom insisted on distributing her most cherished jewelry to the girls before she died, and Dad made sure the boys equally divided the items they had interest in.

When Dad Stewart passed away, Mom Stewart stepped up to the plate and told her children how it would be after she died. She decided who would get the rest of the items, which included silver, china, and several heirloom pieces, by telling them all what her decisions were and that the decisions were final. She documented which charity she wanted used for her clothing, kitchenware, and so on. Mom also made it very clear that none of her children would fight after she left this place, and none of them did. Can you see how Mom Stewart took matters into her own hands and made the decisions for her children so they wouldn't have to? After Mom Stewart passed, the children gathered to divide the estate contents. When they went into the house, it was fairly easy because Mom had already spoken. While there are always some children who will not fulfill the parents' wishes, these children, and most I have worked with, do exactly as their parents asked and come out with a smoother solution than if they didn't.

As you and your siblings go through the process of settling your parents' estate, you can take steps to remove the opportunity for fighting. It is human nature to argue about a strong conviction, and rarely will you see these types of conviction as strongly as in an estate situation where property and cash assets are involved.

This is what I call the *cookies on the table* situation. If your four-year-old daughter sees cookies on the table, she will want them badly and probably take as many as she can fit into her little mouth, especially when you are not looking. You have several options in this situation as a parent. Controlling how many cookies your child consumes is one option ("You may have only two cookies."), or perhaps you take them away altogether, thus reducing the opportunity for further conflict between a stubborn toddler and parent. The child's reaction can be easily predicted: "But I want more! It's not fair!" Such is the case when dividing estate contents or adult cookies.

We must learn to be fair, learn to share, hold hands through the ordeal, and stick close together. Sound elementary? Perhaps, but it's easier said than done. Let's look at some ways you can encourage an attitude of cooperation and kindness among your siblings during this difficult situation.

To Heir Is Human

Throughout the years, many clients and acquaintances have mentioned that the division of their parents' property is beyond grueling. Often we already have ideas in our heads long before the actual estate division of what we would like to have from a loved one's estate. Unfortunately, Murphy's Law often plays a significant part in this process because someone else will always want what you would like to have. This is the exact moment when dividing the property either becomes a roller-coaster ride or a safety net for all involved. If the correct decisions are made ahead of time, most feuding can be avoided or at least diminished greatly. Bumps can be expected along the way, but if each situation is addressed, the ride will go more smoothly.

It is now time for the executor or coexecutors to make some decisions.

Once your parents' debt has been paid (if there is any), the heirs have been notified, and the net worth of your parents is established, the division of the personal property can usually take place. Be sure to ask the attorney handling the estate if it is okay to begin dividing and/or selling the assets.

These decisions and directions will come from the executor, according to the specifications of the will. If there are no specifications, then the executor is supposed to act on the behalf of the estate to make the best decisions possible for that estate. The division of personal property is one of the aspects an executor does not look forward to, and with good reason. Right here is the bulk of the bickering, but it doesn't necessarily have to be this way.

Turning Grief to Joy

Before you begin clearing out your parents' home, think about how you can help keep the process from being contentious. You can't control your siblings' attitudes, but you can control yours and model the kind of generous and cooperative behavior your parents would expect from all of you. It may mean you will have to let go of something you hoped to inherit, but isn't that better than not speaking to your sister for years after your parents are gone?

Before the distribution of your parents' property begins, ask yourself what's really important to you—your dad's stamp collection or honoring your parents' memory by doing everything you can to keep the peace? Grief can bring out the best or the worst in us, and your response to the first disputed object will set the tone for the rest of the process. If your brother makes it clear he wants the gun collection and you had hoped to get it yourself, try to imagine your parents right there in the room with you. Would they want to see you arguing, or would they rather be proud of the generous way you treat each other? Closing out your parents' estate is your last opportunity to honor your parents. As I've emphasized before, this process is all about your parents' wishes, not about yours. If you go into this process with that attitude, it will disarm most potential conflict.

Stay Close

Once you know the value of your parents' belongings and have resolved to honor your parents by being a peacemaker, try to meet privately with your siblings before you begin dividing up the property. Often, families experience real closeness at the funeral, so this would be a good time to build on that. Even if it's just for a few minutes after the dinner that usually accompanies a funeral, meeting face-to-face with your siblings, without any spouses, is a great opportunity to get everyone on the same page: "Hasn't it been great being together again, even with all the sadness of Mom's passing? When we go over to Mom's house in a few weeks to take care of her belongings, let's keep her spirit alive by celebrating the memories that are in that house. And maybe we can all start thinking about that one little thing we'd like to have to remember her." That would also be a good time to let everyone know you're going to have an appraiser identify any items of monetary value and then ask this question: "Should we sell these higher-end items and split the proceeds, or do you think we can divide them fairly between us?" This underscores the reality that equity is the goal and that if everyone cooperates, everyone wins.

An associate of mine whose family divided their parents' estate without incident attributes the success of their experience to this type of meeting. "We were at the viewing before my dad's funeral, and the last guests were leaving when my oldest brother asked my other brothers and me to meet him in the small hospitality room reserved for the family," he told me. "That was the first time we learned that Dad had named him executor of the estate. The first thing he told us was that each of us, along with our children, would be receiving a check that came from the sale of the house and other investments. Then he told us everything in the house was up for grabs and suggested we meet him at a later date and take turns claiming one item at a time that we wanted. Just knowing that ahead of time and being there with the rest of my brothers seemed to put it all in the proper perspective. As it turned out, each of us took about three things and decided the rest should be either sold or donated."

Problems usually begin when someone is left out of the communication loop, which is why I recommend you try to have the initial conversation when your siblings are present for the funeral. And from that time until you return to your parents' house to divide the property, go the extra mile in staying in touch with each other.

Make It a Celebration

At most funerals I've attended, the person officiating begins with a statement like, "We've gathered here to celebrate the life of . . ." Yes, it's always a sad occasion to bid farewell and pay your respects to a departed loved one, but that sadness usually gives way to fond memories and laughter as people share their thoughts and tributes.

Even the difficult and often tedious process of handling the property of your parents can be a continuation of the celebration. So here are some practical suggestions for turning this process into an occasion that brings you closer and honors your parents rather than becoming a battlefield. Don't try to do all of them—just one or two that will serve as icebreakers and subtly remind everyone to focus on your parents instead of themselves.

Start with a tribute. On the appointed day when you and your siblings gather at the family home to divide the contents that aren't covered by the will, don't jump right in with the stuff. Instead, ask everyone to share one quality about your mom or dad that they cherished the most. This keeps the focus on your parents and puts possessions in their proper perspective.

Let your mom and dad join you. Find a nice portrait of your parents and display it in a prominent place. You could even add a lighthearted comment, such as "We all have to be on our best behavior because Mom and Dad are watching our every move, just like when we are kids." Again, this helps to neutralize the "What's in it for me?" mentality.

Listen to the stories behind the objects. Ask everyone to take five minutes and look for one small item that has an interesting story behind it, and then share those stories. This will place the emphasis on the memory of your parents rather than the monetary value of the items.

Give each other a gift. Invite everyone to take a few minutes to look for something you want your siblings to have. Then exchange those gifts, explaining why you chose that particular item. This encourages generosity and gives you a chance to celebrate each other.

Shop for that perfect white elephant. Challenge your siblings to find the most off-the-wall white-elephant gift among the piles of stuff in the house. You'll soon be laughing as everyone takes turns circulating it among the siblings at holidays and special occasions.

Play dress-up. Before you start the process, explain that everyone must find one object of clothing or costume jewelry and wear it as you divide the property. Ridiculous? Sure, that's the point; but it also keeps your parents front and center.

Now that you get the idea, be creative, and find other ways to turn this event into a celebration. If your parents owned a hi-fi, put on some music, preferably old albums from their era. Keep a supply of soft drinks in the fridge and snacks on the counter. This is probably the last time you're all going to be together in your parents' home—possibly the home you grew up in. Keep it lighthearted. Take your time. Imagine how happy your parents would be if they knew you were having a party instead of fighting over a brooch and chipped china.

So what's really in it for you? If you're fortunate, you may discover a few items of significant value that you can sell and come away with a few extra dollars. More likely, you will be able to retrieve items that have great sentimental value to you. Neither of those, however, has any lasting value. What you stand to gain from this final visit to your parents' home is an opportunity to celebrate their lives and grow closer as a family.

Think of the legacy you will leave to your own children if they see you and their aunts and uncles closing out their grandparents' estate in a harmonious, even joyful, manner. I may be an idealist, but I like to think of you driving home after you finally cleared out the house, walking into your living room, and when your teenage daughter asks, "How'd it go, Mom?" you are able to answer, "I had such a nice time with Uncle Dan and Aunt Sherry. It was almost like your grandma and grandpa were there with us."

Tools to Minimize Family Fighting

There are several tools that will clearly minimize fighting if executed appropriately. Many of my clients through the years have shared these techniques, or I have learned them through experience, and they are known to minimize the discomfort for everyone involved. With that said, keep one thing in mind: you cannot please everyone all the time. This is normal and you must accept it up front, but you must also stand by your decisions and be firm with logical reasoning. These techniques should be used when the will specifies that all is to be divided between the children.

Talk with your parents prior to infirmity or death. This conversation is often dreaded by both the older adult as well as the child of the aging parent, but it is absolutely necessary if it is the desire of all involved to communicate freely and openly about the inevitability of what lies ahead in the future. Regardless of whether a family member wants to discuss this, you must make your feelings known either in person or in writing. Be sure to inform or copy all the siblings. "Mom, Dad, please give this serious thought for us. We want to fulfill your wishes first. If you give us the answers to our questions, then no one will have to wonder. Please give this serious consideration, so you don't leave us in the dark about your wishes."

Your parents may be among those who do not want to talk about it and prefer to leave it all up to you, the decision maker. But I can assure you from years of experience, leaving the details of the estate to heirs or children is trying and difficult. Imagine being in a dark forest without a flashlight. This is what it is like without an estate plan; the children are often blindsided by such an overwhelming situation and become resentful because no one guided them through this. I encourage you to go back and read the conversation starters in chapter 2, and start talking with your parents about these issues now.

Approach the division of property with reason and restraint. When dividing your parents' property, whether you are the executor or not, you must realize that some people will always be unreasonable and a challenge to you personally as well as to the process, no matter how much logic you use. You will see behavior that will amaze you. Things might disappear, locks might be changed, wills might go AWOL, or the shy sister suddenly develops a bad case of "gimme, gimme, gimme." Do your best to arm yourself with logical reasons and techniques. Your siblings may disagree and put up a fight, but they cannot say you are being unfair or dishonest. If they hurt you, do your best to turn the other cheek. In the long run, it is what it is, and it is not worth fighting over. Ultimately, you can't take it with you either.

During this entire process, all types of communication should be documented. Regardless of whether your family is prone to feuding, all communication about the estate should be documented, copied, and distributed to the family. For example, include everyone in all e-mails, make sure everyone gets a copy of the appraiser's report, and so on. Document every phone call by keeping a journal.

Call a family meeting where all of the heirs can gather at the same time either in person or via teleconference. Do this so everyone can clearly see that they are all on the same page at the same time. (As I have said earlier, this first meeting should include immediate heirs only—not spouses. This is necessary to simplify the situation.) This playing field must be refereed at all times, usually by the executor, and usually by documenting everything to everyone. This meeting will establish a starting point for the division of estate items and offer the heirs the order in which the process will go. The next step is to create a wish list for each heir.

Create a wish list. If your parents did not leave a master list, encourage every heir to write a wish list of what they would like to have from the estate. This is not a guarantee they will get the item(s) they choose; it is only a wish list. Please make sure this is clear to them. If the will calls for equal distribution of assets, then you will ask each sibling (at the same time and in the same way) to send you their wish lists. Do not include grandchildren at this point—just immediate heirs only. If your siblings want to include items for the grandchildren on their lists, that is fine, but that will take the place of one of their choices. Be sure to give everyone a date for the wish list to be completed. For example, "I must have your wish list by September 18 at the latest, or we will have to proceed without you."

Hire a personal property appraiser. An appraiser can assign values to the items on the wish lists and anything else of value in the home. These values in this appraisal report will be put with the items on each heir's wish list. Once the appraiser has completed the task of assessing the contents and values, place the appraiser's report with the wish list and combine the two documents for your soon-to-be spreadsheet. Having an appraiser formally document values is imperative to the process. For one, it gives you a fair and objective viewpoint of what things are really worth, regardless of family stories. Second, be very careful doing any valuation on your own accord. The IRS has penalties for underevaluation of estate items, so it's best to let a professional give you a completely unbiased opinion. If someone in the family does it, this can be, and often is, misconstrued to lean the value one way or another. An objective third party creates a safe place for all.

Create a spreadsheet. Once you receive all the wish lists back from the heirs, create a single document listing everyone's name and items they would like to have. Give each heir a column with his or her name on top and the list of items below it. Leave a space to the side of the item where you can later insert a value once you receive the appraisal report. This is necessary for keeping it fair.

Once you know the values of the major home contents, it is time to fill in the blanks by combining all the names, wishes, and values of all the siblings or heirs. (See the sample wish list spreadsheet in appendix D.)

If You All Want the Same Item

If after creating your original spreadsheet you discover that Greg and Joe and Anne and Barbara all want the same item, you have several options. First, on a separate sheet of paper, document all the common wants (sisters both want the silver; brothers both want all the guns, and so on). Once documented, have an uninterested party flip a coin, draw straws, pull names out of a hat, or assist you and your siblings to compromise or trade. Or you could consider sharing the contested items by passing them around throughout the year, as mentioned in chapter 6.

If you can't do any of the above, sell the item quickly so it does not remain a bone of contention, and divide the proceeds by the number of interested siblings. Distribute the proceeds in a very timely manner—do not delay because they will grow restless.

Do everything you can to solve these contested situations creatively rather than legally. It would be extremely painful to have a cherished family heirloom's fate decided by the courts—perhaps directed to be sold and the proceeds divided between the unwavering parties. When that happens, the heirloom is lost forever to future generations.

When the final decisions are made, document them in the margin of the spreadsheet for a permanent record.

Financial Equivalence

The goal is to get everyone as close as possible to having the same financial totals on the spreadsheet. Use the appraisal report, and apply the value to the item(s) on the wish lists. If Rob wants the grandfather clock, then under Rob's column on the spreadsheet, put "Grandfather clock: $1,200," or if Susie wants the antique sewing machine, then "Sewing machine: $175," and so on for each sibling or heir. It's fine if Jane wants the antique silver, but what if its value is far higher than anyone realizes? Would it be fair for her to receive a $12,000 silver set and another sibling to get a $500 desk? Not really. This is how fights start. So let's extinguish this fire before it even gets started. Keep it fair, simple, and equal. If the totals are unbalanced, then every effort must be made to make them equal. At the end of each column will be the final tally. You will see the differences; there is always one who wants more than others, and it would appear one or two may not want much.

Is it possible to make everyone happy all the time? I'm not sure it is. There will always be differences in the number of items a sibling desires as well as the dollar amount siblings will choose. Some siblings choose only the highest-dollar items just because they are worth the most, whether they like them or not. And there will be those who only want Mom's spectacles or inexpensive wedding band. Since siblings can often be at opposite ends of the spectrum, besides following my earlier advice of keeping an accurate spreadsheet of who wants what and the estimated value of the items, I recommend the following.

When the spreadsheet is complete and everyone's information is in black and white for all to see, tally each sibling's column and show the final dollar amount for each. If Rebecca's wish list is tallied at $13,000, and Ron's tally is up to $1,600, we need to find a way to make it up to Ron. Normally, that way is by means of cash assets. Making up the difference in money would be the correct approach. Or a family might say, "Ron, which would you prefer: cash or Mom's car?" Just make sure it is fair and objective.

Some families do not mind if one sibling gets more than another, and that is fine too. I am just giving you the tools you may need to prevent feelings from getting hurt. Occasionally, siblings will say they don't mind or don't care, only to have their resentment and anger escalate as the years pass and eventually show their true colors at a most inopportune time, such as a family Christmas party. We want to prevent that too.

Another option is to have each heir's tally removed from his or her bottom-line cash inheritance and placed back into the estate pot, and then deduct the cash from those totals equally among children. Let's say that each child is to get $100,000 in cash. If Jack only wants $1,000 in stuff, but his sister wants $20,000 worth of stuff, simply deduct their totals from their $100,000 inheritance. It still goes back into the estate but cuts into their portion of cash. While this is a very businesslike manner of dividing an estate and may turn some people off, it is highly thought of by many. It is completely fair to place the money back into the hands of the heirs, and it actually controls some from taking the lion's share. If the siblings want something, they can pay for it out of their inheritance.

Naturally, if the will specifies an item for a child or friend, then that item should be given freely to that person without any controversy at all from others. However, this should be proven in writing, not just a person claiming, "Mom wanted me to have that." Putting things in writing is the best preventive strategy to avoid future problems.

Decide on a date that all siblings or heirs must be present in the home for the actual division of property. You can expect tensions to be high, but you are only hours away from getting through this challenging time. It would be nice if you thought to bring some coffee or refreshments. Soft music in the background is also advisable. And to avoid a battle right from the start, use a fair method of deciding who goes first: birth order, flip of a coin, names drawn from a hat.

Fast Facts

- The most likely person to exploit the elderly is a family member or someone familiar to them.

- 60 percent of those financially abusing the elderly are adult children (National Elder Abuse Incidence Study).

- The cost of contesting a will often depletes the value of the property being contested.

- Five million cases of financial abuse of the elderly are reported each year (NPR).

- 1.1 percent of Americans receive $50,000 to $100,000 in inheritance; 1.1 percent receive more than $100,000; 91.9 percent receive nothing.[1]

What About Fights that Break Out?

It is important to remember to keep in mind that someone else's actions have little to do with you personally. It has everything to do with what is going on inside of that person with his own private issues. There is no magical formula to dissolve all fighting. Here's one technique that seems to calm down everyone:

1. Clearly identify who is the bearer of the problem.

2. Remain calm and say to that person, "Let's make sure we understand the problem. Tell me why you are so upset, and give me two or three possible solutions to this problem as you see it." You must remain calm at all times through this process. Place not only the problem on the dissenter's lap but also the possible solution.

3. Become a master of delegation. My guess is this person expects someone else to figure out the solution to his problem. Once he offers possible solutions, openly discuss them with the others who

are present. Everyone should agree on the best approach. After a solution is agreed upon, put this problem where it belongs: behind all of you.

4. Don't look back, and don't allow anyone else to drag this issue back into the conversation once everyone agrees on a solution. Once it's a done deal, keep moving forward.

A Word About Fighting

It has been my experience that many fights that break out during the process of settling an estate are either misunderstandings that require open communication or an event that has remained embedded in the mind of a sibling, festering for many years, just waiting for this chance to blast a family member (as in, "You were always Dad's favorite, and I got left in the dust!"). Holding on to a grudge will hurt you far more than the targeted person and feel like an anchor around your neck. So why hold on to your grudge if it continually pulls you down?

In the case where it involves a misunderstanding, the two or more parties (and a mediator, if you feel more comfortable) must sit down together in person and express all the hard feelings. Get everything out on the table. Even if you are deeply hurt by the situation, put your feelings and the situation on the table, and say it as nicely as you can. Harsh words will only cause defenses to rise, and then those walls will prove impenetrable.

Some people would rather go on with their hard feelings than admit their hurt or deep pain. Therefore, they may not be willing to discuss the issue. I encourage gentle nudging to make sure the issue is acknowledged and relieved. A kind, loving letter can often do wonders to soften a bitter heart. If the person chooses not to read it, then that issue belongs to him or her, not you. You did your part by reaching out the best you knew how. What I am hoping you will glean from this is that you can walk into or out of a situation knowing you have done all that you can do to the best of your ability. This will enable you to walk with your head high the rest of your life, knowing you did all you could regardless of how the other person involved accepts it.

If a fight breaks out during the process of settling your parents' estate, here are a few other things you can do to help your family member deal with and overcome her bitterness or grudge.

Validate feelings. Tell the person something like, "I do see your point now and feel badly you have felt this way for years. Now that I know, what do you think we should do to heal this?" Hear what the person is saying, feel what she is saying, do your best to understand her, and then find a way to nurture the situation.

Listen to the person's pain. Most of the time, all the person wants is to be heard. But a word of warning: draw clear boundaries here. Do not let the person go on and on throughout the process. Air it out, and continue to move forward.

Encourage everyone to be a part of the process. Like a well-oiled machine, a team player will do much to help this situation, but if a part is missing or gets clogged up, the whole process slows down or stops altogether. For the best results, you and your siblings need to work as a team.

After everyone decides who gets what and all the bumps and challenges are ironed out, conclude the meeting by deciding on a date for all siblings or heirs to be present in the home for moving day. Decide on a day and time that the assets have to be moved out. Allot enough time so everyone can get fair airfares, arrange for moving services, and so on. I recommend that all the siblings and heirs come and do this on the same day. Now that everything has been divided, it is okay to send a representative in your place if you cannot be present. This way, every heir can clearly see all is fair, and no one is making off with so much as an extra crumb!

Dividing your parents' possessions can bring out either the best or the worst in you and your siblings. It's such an emotional experience that sometimes we just can't help ourselves. By following the counsel in this chapter, you may not completely eliminate family squabbles, but you will reduce the number of those disagreements and find ways to live gracefully with the rest.

What Do I Do Now?

Current situation: your last surviving parent has passed away.

☑ *Locate the will.* This document will guide you through the distribution process, among other things.

☑ *Arrange for a meeting with your siblings.* Even if it's just a few minutes after the viewing or funeral, set a time when you and your siblings can meet briefly to plan the next steps.

☑ *Plan for the distribution of property.* With your siblings, create a plan for when you will all return to the family home to begin the distribution process.

☑ *Stay in touch.* Take it upon yourself to maintain frequent communication with your siblings prior to the distribution of property and clearing out of the house.

Nine

But What Is It *Really* Worth?

Several years ago, an older gentleman wandered through one of my estate sales for more than three hours. Quiet and keeping to himself, he posed no threat or worry to me or anyone else. I just figured he was taking his time making a decision, like many of the other customers. Perhaps he was even interested in the real estate, a nice three-bedroom home located on a large corner lot. I'm often able to sell the house on the day of the estate sale and thought it would be nice for my client if we could wrap everything up in one day.

Finally the man approached me with a question: "How much is that crepe myrtle in the front yard?"

I didn't quite know how to answer. "You mean that thirty-foot tree in the yard?" I asked.

"That's right," he answered. "How much do you want for it?"

"Well, sir, that would be $260,000 because that's the price of the house. Unfortunately, I can't remove anything from the grounds since it's part of the real estate. So if you want the tree, you have to buy the whole place."

It wasn't the answer he wanted, so he persisted, telling me he was perfectly capable of digging up the tree and hauling it away and that he didn't see how that would affect the sale of the property. I assured him I knew it would be relatively easy for him to take away the tree but that I didn't have the authority to let him do it. He looked disappointed but turned without a word and continued wandering through the house for another two hours. I went back to answering questions from other customers until once again he approached me, this time carrying an old toilet seat that he had unscrewed from a commode. He had it looped over his arm, much like a woman would carry her purse.

"How much for this?" he asked without the slightest hint that he was doing anything out of the ordinary. I was flabbergasted but tried my best to keep my poker face. How do you put a value on a used toilet seat? What kind of person would wrestle it off a commode? What use could he possibly have for it?

As I stood there momentarily speechless, he reached into his pocket and pulled out three crumpled dollar bills and handed them to me. "Here you go, honey," he said as he turned to leave before I could decide if I should sell it or not. "You have a nice day, now."

You just never know what things people consider valuable, so in this chapter I'd like to take you inside the mind of an appraiser to help you understand what might have value in your parents' home and why. But remember, ultimately something is worth what someone is willing to give you for it.

In this chapter, I will help you make some initial decisions about the potential value of some of your parents' possessions. This information will help you set aside things of sentimental and monetary value and lead to a more timely (and peaceful) dissolution of your parents' estate. If you suspect that your parents' estate might include something of value, you really need to have it appraised. I will explain how you can do that in the next chapter, but for now I want to stress that it would be unwise to try to sell any item of potential value without an appraisal. Typically, a family will discover a valuable antique and might take it straight to a dealer. The family might not have an idea what it's worth and usually takes whatever is offered.

It's Probably Just Junk

Susan called me one summer afternoon as I was enjoying a glass of iced tea. She explained that her father had died a few weeks ago, leaving her the sole beneficiary of his estate. "He collected so many things over the years, and I have no idea what to do with them," she explained. "I doubt that any of it is valuable, but I don't even know where to start."

It's probably the most common business call I receive, and I always accept these assignments with anticipation because I've learned over the years that most homes contain at least one little surprise that's as much fun for me to discover as it is for the relative to enjoy. Susan's case was no exception.

After winding through the countryside for several miles, I couldn't believe my eyes when I arrived at the address. I was expecting an old farmhouse or at least a pleasant little home in the country, but leaning to one side before me was a tiny, crooked white house that looked as if it had been abandoned years ago. As I double-checked my directions to make sure I was at the right place, a woman who appeared to be in her forties walked out the front door and introduced herself as Susan. Sure enough, this was the estate Susan wanted me to appraise.

What I discovered inside gave credence to the adage "Don't judge a book by its cover." This tiny, lopsided shack turned out to be a showplace of museum-quality pieces. Stunned, I made my way through the house, carefully handling the many artifacts that Susan had already set out for me, and then opening box after box of other amazing collectibles. But the real surprise came when I went through her father's collection of books. I scanned through the five or six hundred books, selecting ten that warranted further research. Finally it was time for me to return to my home office and begin the research, and I must admit I raced home to see what sort of treasure I had stumbled upon.

Eager to get to my desk, I pulled out my reference books and nearly fell off my chair when I learned the value of the first book: $22,000! The other nine books had a total value of $5,000, and Susan was ecstatic when I called her with the news.

Now I'll admit this doesn't happen very often. But I share this story because so many times my clients begin their phone calls with, "I'm pretty sure none of the stuff my parents left behind is worth very much." And it makes me wonder about all those people who never get a professional appraisal and either throw away most of their parents' "junk" or donate it to a company that doesn't even know its value. I can just imagine some unsuspecting bargain shopper buying an old picture just for the frame, throwing away the painting that might be worth several thousand dollars. It happens.

Two Types of Value

Sometimes a piece doesn't have much monetary value, but it does have priceless sentimental value to a child. When Sharon was a little girl, her mother sat beside her on her bed each night and brushed her long, brown hair. As she brushed, they talked about everything that moms and daughters talk about: what happened at school that day, the boy who always picked on her, all the whys, like "Why do teachers always assign homework on weekends?" Her mom would tuck her in, pull the covers up around her neck, and then say a little prayer they had memorized.

It made sense that of all the things her mother left behind after she passed away, Sharon went straight for the brush that her mother kept and used on her own hair after Sharon left for college. That brush wasn't an antique, nor was it made out of some exotic material that would give it monetary value. It was probably purchased at a Woolworth's for less than five dollars. But to Sharon, it was invaluable because it brought back all those wonderful times when she had her mom all to herself. The brush held no monetary value, but it was loaded with sentimental value, and in Sharon's eyes, it was priceless.

As you go through your parents' home to divide its belongings among your family members, you should first look for those items that carry special meaning. But I always caution my clients to exercise some discrimination and restraint because if you're not careful, you will haul away a trailer full of stuff that ultimately will just be stashed away someplace where it will have no value at all. For Sharon, the brush will sit on her own dresser and remind her each day of her mother. Usually, two or three items that have sentimental value are all you need. Look for those things that have special meaning and that can either be displayed where you will see them or can actually be used. For example, if you used to go fishing with your dad, taking one of his fishing poles and actually using it occasionally is a wonderful way to recall all those fun fishing trips.

Sentimental value may even be the highest value for some people. Within a year of the funeral, any money you may have received from the sale of your parents' property will either have been spent or added to your mutual fund. But those few items you retrieve that carry sentimental value will be with you forever, keeping your parents' memories alive for you, your family, and your friends.

Still, when most people face the daunting task of dividing the property of their parents' home, they see dollar signs. On the one hand there very well could be items of significant value, just like the pair of vases I found in the family's intended Goodwill pile, which I sold for $57,500. This can and does happen and is a wonderful example of *monetary* value and why you need an appraiser! But more often than not, the average estate sale brings in between $6,000 and $20,000, with the majority being around $8,000 to $10,000. In my experience, I've found that most people are disappointed at the limited monetary value of the things their parents left behind. So let's begin looking at some of the factors that influence or affect monetary value.

Antique, Vintage, Collectible?

When discussing the monetary value of items, consider whether they are antique, vintage, or collectible. Though these terms have complex meanings and effect on value, here is a brief overview:

- *Antique* refers to an item that is at least one hundred years old.
- *Vintage* describes older items that are not yet one hundred years old. Generally, vintage items are seen in antique stores and considered collectible. Vintage pieces are original to the period that produced them and not reproductions.

- *Collectible* refers to anything people collect, usually older items on their way to becoming antique.

These terms are often misunderstood and improperly used. When determining the value of any item, it is always best to consult a professional appraiser.

The Law of Supply and Demand

Let us return to basic economics for a moment. The law of supply and demand pretty much sets the standard for everything, everywhere, at all times. Too much supply causes prices to go down, and higher demand forces the prices upward. At higher prices, suppliers will wish to sell more, but consumers will wish to buy less. At lower prices, consumers will wish to buy more, but suppliers will be willing to sell less. Supply and demand work together to determine the price of everything.

We must also understand demand in order to understand the market. Demand is influenced by the desire of the market, the ability to pay for it, and the willingness to pay for it.

Marketability. Remember Beanie Babies? Back in the early 1990s, these stuffed animals were the rage, often selling out because they were so popular. Today, there is a small market for them, but not the demand there was several years ago. Sometimes you can find them stacked on tables at garage sales. What happened? The demand for them decreased. When they were the new, hot item on the market, this desire created a demand for the product. Then the supply met that demand over the course of time, and the demand for the little critters decreased. Most items, whether they are hot or cool on the market, seem to have collectors. You just have to find them.

Marketability is a term that describes the relative demand for a specific item. For example, a decade or so ago, Depression glass was quite desirable, but today there is not as much demand for it, and prices are on the lower side. Antiques will always hold the attention of many casual buyers, but professional collectors pay attention to the strength of the market. They know what's hot and what's not and watch the market as they make their purchases. You may discover a lovely set of silver candlesticks that *should* be valuable, but if the market for silver has taken a dip (which it has in recent years but is showing signs of slowly coming back up), those candlesticks will not have as much monetary value as you anticipated until the market changes. Watching market trends is one of the jobs of an appraiser.

Collectibility. Somewhat related to marketability, if an item belongs to a category of objects that people desire and therefore collect, it could increase its value. This can be tricky because what's collectible today could plummet tomorrow. Conversely, something of limited value could become a collectible due to historical factors. For example, prior to NASCAR champion Dale Earnhardt's tragic death, #3 Earnhardt souvenirs were worth basically what you paid for them. The day after his death, the Internet site eBay carried more than one hundred thousand Earnhardt items, selling quickly for very high prices. Ultimately, it is the collector who will set the values in the marketplace.

Age. Many older adults and baby boomers believe that because a lot of their possessions are old, they must be worth a lot of money. I always remind my clients that just because something is old, it doesn't necessarily mean that it is valuable. This is another strong reason for hiring a professional appraiser for an objective valuation. Where I live, I see a lot of Victorian period furniture. It's a distinct style and is grand to look at, but it generally does not sell for much unless you have a very unique piece. I also tell my clients that old junk is still junk—every generation has its share of cheap products that do not gain value with age.

Does age play a role in the value of an item? Absolutely! Age is a contributing factor, but it does not stand alone. You should set aside anything that you even suspect has value or age to be looked at by a professional. Today, even our childhood toys from the '50s and '60s are considered collectible and desirable. Just look at Barbie and GI Joe! There are several other factors that affect the value of items, which will become clear in the following pages.

Condition. Through the millennia, people have been refurbishing, repairing, restoring, recreating, repainting, reshaping, replating, and repolishing things to make them look shiny and new. But if it is an antique item, it is not supposed to look shiny and new because it's *old*. If we were 120 years old, don't you think we would look a bit strange trying to look fifteen again? Remember, the age of a piece brings with it qualities that collectors look for and usually include age-related indicators, such as the mellowness of the original wood that has not been refinished, natural darkening of the leather, and so on. To strip an antique of its original surface interrupts the natural aging process of the piece.

Serious differentials can occur in pricing when it comes to a beautiful antique piece of furniture that is in good original condition and one that has been refinished. The true collector will choose an untouched original piece every time, providing the condition of the overall piece is good. Nicks, scrapes, and dings are all part of the item's history and personality and somewhat expected on an antique piece.

With metal objects, such as bronze or brass, part of their antique value also comes from patina, a chemical compound formed on the surface of metals from exposure to the elements. If you find an old bronze lamp and use some metal polish to clean it up and make it look brand-new, you will have rubbed away some of its monetary value.

Many older adults like metal items in their homes to be shiny and bright. I usually instruct all my clients to leave bronze and copper alone. That two-hundred-year-old molasses pot should look two hundred years old, and someday that patina will add to the value of that piece. It's what collectors look for—proof that the piece really is that old. If you have nineteenth-century bronzes, polishing them will not only make them look new and somewhat odd, but you will erase a century or more of time and the elements that made those pieces earn their age. You have interrupted the natural aging process, which diminishes the value and aesthetic beauty to a true connoisseur of fine antique objects.

Take the Statue of Liberty, for example. The green surface you see today is the natural patination process of the copper being exposed to the elements since 1886. Imagine if we didn't like the way she looked and sent out a bunch of polishing people to make her look shiny and new again. Lady Liberty wouldn't look quite right, would she? My point is she is not supposed to look new because she isn't new. She is a welcome sight for thousands and has been so for nearly a century. Leaving her as she is, green and all, is the best way to treat her. She's proud of her age.

This brings to mind a lovely elderly woman who produced a fabulous eighteenth-century Chinese export piece only to proudly show me the hole she just had the local handyman drill in the bottom of the vase to make a pretty lamp. And a pretty lamp it made, but the problem was that the gorgeous vase lost a large bit of its value for two reasons. First, the original condition of the piece has been forever altered. It is no longer a vase, which was the original intent for the piece. Second, the vase is now permanently damaged with the hole in it. When in doubt about an item, leave it alone, as close to its original condition as possible.

In the 1970s, a lot of people—probably your parents included—bought old furniture and took it to a business to strip it clean of all the old paint and varnish. Then they would painstakingly try to restore the piece to its original condition, carefully staining it and applying multiple shiny coats of varnish or polyurethane and even giving it the distressed look. Unfortunately, the worst thing you can do with old furniture from a collector's point of view is to strip it.

Rarity. Rarity is relative. The definition of *rare* is "extraordinary—beyond what is ordinary or usual." Many people think what they have in their homes is rare, but what they may have instead are unusual or unique items. An example of a rare item would be a flawless diamond (no inclusions) with no color (colorless). To find this diamond is possible, but the cost would be significantly higher than an average diamond because it is much harder to find. The earth simply didn't make as many of these perfect stones! Ultimately, the scarcity or rarity of an item is directly relational to how many people want it and are willing to buy it.

If you have one rare item and one hundred people want it, the price will skyrocket. But if you have three rare items and no one wants them, the demand is not there, and the price will not be very high.

One time when I was speaking to a group about the potential value of their estates, an elderly lady stood up and announced she owned a belt buckle that actually belonged to Robert E. Lee. Such an item would be a treasure anywhere, but here in the South it would be akin to the Holy Grail. So of course I asked her if she had any proof that it actually belonged to General Lee. She replied, "Of course I have proof! The initials R.E.L. are engraved on it, and my daddy told me it belonged to him." Unfortunately, that's not enough proof to validate the belt buckle. Even if there was such a buckle, the value would be dependent on being able to prove it is a historically significant piece, in addition to market comparisons and expert opinions. If you claim an item is rare and valuable, you must have proof. Hearsay is not enough.

In the world of antiques, we have a word we use to measure the validity or proven history of an item: *provenance*. The definition of *provenance* is the record or history of past ownership of an item that must be documented with paperwork, signatures, photographic proof (a picture that places the item in an historic period), or other evidence.

Professional comparables may include auction records and other documented sales that compare similar items within a similar time period, expert opinions, research and documented records, and test results, all of which are often used to help establish provenance. If you own a uniform of New York Yankees' Joe DiMaggio, you own something of value. If you have provenance to go with it—a letter signed by Joe indicating he donated it to someone, along with a photo of him with Marilyn Monroe while he's wearing it, for example—you have a fabulous find! Provenance could be the difference between a hundred-dollar antique rifle and a rifle owned and used by Wild Bill Hickok.

Material. What something is made of also affects its value. Exotic wood furniture is generally more valuable than a more common wood such as pine or oak. Genuine gemstones bring a higher price than costume jewelry. Then there are those rare materials that will always have value: gold, platinum, diamonds, sterling silver, ivory, coral, fine jade, exceptional furniture with fine marquetry and craftsmanship, carvings, and so on.

A rarer quality material might also indicate superior craftsmanship, therefore keeping the values higher because they were made to last.

Style. Furniture styles have come and gone through the ages, much like ladies' hairstyles: some are classic, and some are fads. The same is true of furniture. Through the centuries, some furniture has become obsolete because it is too large or too uncomfortable, losing its functionality. Some prefer the simplicity of antique primitive or Danish Modern furniture while others desire the grandiose presence of American Empire period pieces. Still others will prefer the formal style of French Provincial or ornate style of rococo pieces. Whichever style is popular at the time affects the value of the piece. When the demand for a specific furniture style is low, the price decreases. When the demand goes up, the price increases.

Handmade versus factory made. Handmade items are more valuable than factory made, but sometimes even the experts can be fooled. About a year ago I was asked by an elderly woman to appraise her belongings so her children would know the value of her possessions after she died. When I walked through the door of her home, I saw the most exquisite wooden desk. Every feature added to the value: mid-nineteenth century, Dutch marquetry, mixed woods, and beautiful craftsmanship. I was up to $20,000 in no time. Upon closer inspection, I was even more impressed. The workmanship of the inlaid woods was spectacular: phoenixes, fleur-de-lis, urns, and so on. I lifted the top to reveal twenty miniature drawers, each with ivory handles and several pigeonholes with a couple of secret compartments. I pulled out a few drawers to see how they were constructed, and one of them contained a handwritten note glued to the side, easily looked to be mid-1800s material. In short, it was an absolutely beautiful piece that anyone would be proud to own.

I photographed the writing up close and e-mailed it to a colleague of mine who is very good at researching written language such as this and was humbled by his reply. The little note translated into "Factory made in Belgium." It turned out to be a piece made for export, and the value of my estimate dropped from $20,000 to $8,000. It was still a gorgeous piece, but not what I originally thought.

Collectible, Vintage, and Antique Items that May Have Value

Here is a brief list of some of the types of things you should look for in your parents' estate when trying to isolate antique or vintage items of value or collectibles that have remained consistent in the market. (This is only the tip of the iceburg.) You should have them all looked at by a personal property appraiser.

Advertising items (signs, posters, giveaways)
Art—paintings, lithographs, and sculptures (signed, original)
Barbie dolls
Baseball cards/sports memorabilia
Black Americana
Books (first editions and leather, some antique)
Cameras and other photographic equipment
Christmas items
Clothing
Coin and stamp collections
Cookie jars
Crystal (antique/signed)
Dolls and accessories
Early electric fans
Fishing lures
Fountain pens
Furniture
European figurines (especially German and English)
Glassware
Guns
Inkwells
Jewelry (costume, signed pieces, and genuine jewelry)

Kitchenware
Lace/crochet work
Ladies' compacts/perfumes/vanity items
Lamps
Linens
Lionel trains (original)
Mantel clocks and long case clocks
Movie posters
Paperweights, preferably signed near base or on bottom
Photos
Pocket watches, railroad or genuine gold
Porcelain plates, hand painted
Postcards
Primitives (folk art)
Quilts
Radios
Railroad memorabilia
Rugs
Sterling silver, gold, and platinum
Tapestries, textiles, and samplers
Tobaccoiana (smoking collectibles)
Tools
Toys
War/military memorabilia

If You Think It's a Treasure

One last thought on potential value. Remember Susan and the $22,000 book? Based on my research, that was an accurate appraisal of this rare book, but not the actual selling price. I had contacted a book dealer who specializes in botanical books and eventually sold the book to him for $17,500, which still thrilled Susan even though it was less than my appraisal. What happened? Remember, the optimum value was $22,000, and we were selling it to a dealer—a broker who will in turn sell it on the open market. He will most likely set the price around $22,000, and the difference between what he paid Susan and what he will sell it for is what keeps him in business. Susan could have tried to sell it herself to an individual buyer, but without any experience or contacts in the world of rare books, it could have taken her a year or more to sell, or she would not have made that much.

Since we knew the value of the book, she could make an informed decision on what a fair offer was. My point is this: never sell an item of significant value (or perceived value) without having it professionally appraised. The cost of an appraisal will always pay for itself.

You'll notice there weren't any Cool Whip containers on that list. Or old magazines, jars of buttons, spools of thread, or canning jars. In most homes, greater than 50 percent of the things that have accumulated over the years can either be donated or go straight to the Dumpster. Now that you know the difference between the stuff to keep and the stuff to get rid of, you're ready to tackle the house.

What Do I Do Now?

Current situation: anytime, but especially prior to clearing out your parents' home.

☑ *Locate the property list.* If your parents already had their property appraised, find the appraisal report. If it is greater than five years old, have another appraisal done on the property for updated values.

☑ *Negotiate the sentimental items.* Ask each sibling to identify the things of sentimental value he or she would like to keep.

☑ *Identify items of potential monetary value.* Using the property list if your parents had one, note any items you think may have monetary value. If your parents did not have a list, visit the home and take inventory.

☑ *Keep talking.* From the time of the funeral until the actual estate liquidation, do your best to maintain good communication with your siblings and all others involved.

Ten

Where Do I Begin?

Margaret called me from a Chicago suburb with a frantic tone in her voice. "We have all this stuff, and we don't have a clue how to get rid of it! It looks like it might be junk, but there are some antiques in here too. What do we do? My mom has a friend who is sort of in the business. She's dabbled in buying and selling for years. Maybe I should just hire her."

Her words "My mom has a friend . . . sort of in the business . . . who dabbles in buying and selling" hit a nerve. It's sort of like saying, "My brother got an A in dissecting, so why not let him do your brain surgery?"

I strongly urged her to hire a professional, warning her about letting a well-intentioned but untrained friend handle something as important as this. But she decided to go to her friend anyway, a decision that cost her dearly.

A month later, Margaret called me again in tears. "I've made a horrible mistake, and I don't know how to undo it. My mom's friend didn't know the true value of many of the items in the house and sold them for pennies. One local dealer contacted me to tell me the estate person charged seventy-five dollars for a fine antique English Windsor chair that was worth about eight hundred, and an antique needlepoint sampler dated 1854 sold for ten dollars but should have sold for several hundred. I am eaten up with misery wondering how many other things got sold for next to nothing."

Throughout this book, I have recommended that you get help for the various duties you will need to perform during the process of settling your parents' estate. I have also cautioned you to make sure you get the right kind of help. Unfortunately, unscrupulous professionals come out of the woodwork in times of crisis, and you can easily fall victim to their dishonest and unethical practices. In this brief chapter, I will help you determine the assistance you will need and give you some guidance for finding trustworthy professionals.

Before we begin, here are some general guidelines. As with any commercial transaction, you get what you pay for when it comes to professional help. If you think hiring a professional is expensive, try hiring an amateur. To save money, many people will turn to a friend—or a friend of a friend—who is a lawyer or other professional, or someone who dabbles in this or that. I recommend against this for two reasons. First, family dynamics are difficult enough to negotiate, and if you hire a friend to help with any part of the process, you will unknowingly increase suspicions that you are trying to protect your own interests. Second, the friend may not be adequately qualified or informed to give you the help you need. For example, your husband's golfing buddy may be an attorney, but his practice is mostly in personal injury law. Sure, he's been to law school and is licensed to practice in your state, but he may have limited knowledge of your parents' particular estate situation. I have found that the money spent to hire the right professional is rarely questioned and provides peace of mind. Better to be safe than sorry.

Regardless of whom you consider to help you, always ask for and check references. If you're hiring an appraiser, ask for the names of a couple of previous clients, attorneys, or banks, and call them to see if they were pleased with their appraisal work. Also, it goes without saying that the professional you hire needs to be properly insured and, where available, certified by a professional organization.

Helper Checklist

- Find a local attorney to assist with the will or any other matters relating to your parents' property.
- Know the names of any institutions where your parents had investments.

- Contact your parents' homeowners' insurance company agent about any changes in the policy after the contents of the home are removed and it is vacant pending sale.

- List the home with a local Realtor if it is to be sold.

- Hire a certified personal property appraiser to assess the value of the home's contents and determine if an estate sale is recommended.

- Make sure you have adequate help with the actual removal of the home's contents.

- Secure the use of a truck or a hauling service if larger items need to be moved to other locations.

- Notify your pastor or rabbi of your situation.

- Have at least one close friend or counselor to help you cope with the grief and stress.

Helping Your Parents Find the Right Professionals

If your parents are still alive and mentally strong, I highly recommend that you help them find a financial planner who specializes in working with senior citizens. A financial planner will look over all your parents' assets—pension, 401(k) plans, Social Security benefits, and real estate—and make recommendations to help maximize those assets and minimize tax liabilities. In the simplest of terms, they make recommendations so that your parents will not run out of money before they die and will have something left over for either their families or charity. They will also show them how to avoid leaving more to the IRS than they need to, usually through setting up trusts. They may also recommend that your parents consolidate their assets with one or two institutions. According to one financial planner I interviewed, it's not unusual for seniors to have money in twenty to thirty different accounts, which is not only confusing to them (because they receive pages of reports each quarter), but it also wreaks havoc on survivors who have to settle all those accounts.

An estate planning attorney does a lot more than help to create a will. He will discuss issues and scenarios your parents may have never even considered. He will help them think through and arrange for their wishes to be fulfilled if something should happen to them. Estate planning attorneys will also help to minimize taxes and fees and plan for health care wishes if a parent no longer can speak for himself. This plan offers a set of directions for the individual(s) chosen to carry out these wishes when a person is no longer able.

Most likely, the estate planning attorney and financial planner might recommend an appraisal of your parents' property and possessions, so your parents will need to contact a real estate appraiser for the real property and a personal property appraiser for the residential contents. Since this is my discipline, naturally I support this recommendation so that your parents know what they have and can make decisions about those things before they die. However, I caution you to make sure that an uninterested party is hired—meaning, the appraiser has no desire to purchase the item(s). Your parents should make it clear to the appraiser that they are not interested in selling anything being appraised but want the appraisal to make decisions for their heirs. I personally believe that an appraiser should remain at all times an uninterested, objective third party whose foremost obligation is to report the truth while upholding a code of ethics.

Another professional you may want to help your parents consult with is a funeral director. You would be surprised how many elderly people die without having made arrangements for their funerals, burials, or cemetery plots, leaving the family scrambling to make arrangements because they never shared their final wishes. Many funeral homes now offer advance payment options so the financial burden as well as difficult decisions at the time of death are minimized. Lately, many of my older clients have shared with me that they have made plans for their funerals and left specific instructions for their children.

Many older adults avoid meeting with these professionals for two reasons: first, they do not want to confront their own mortality, and second, they are on fixed incomes and do not think they can afford the costs involved. Your gentle persuasion is all I can recommend for getting them to seek help in these matters. As for the cost, it is true that some of these professionals might have fees that are a little steep for a person on a fixed income. It would be a kind and helpful gesture if you and your siblings are able to chip in to cover this cost if you feel that would not offend your parents.

If liquidating your parents' estate includes selling their home, I highly recommend using a Realtor rather than trying to sell the house yourself. There is no shortage of Realtors, so select one of the more prominent ones, and explain that you are selling the home of a deceased parent. In addition to listing and showing the home, they can help you with other details, such as making sure the title is free, determining the status of property taxes, and suggesting any changes you may need to make on the house insurance policy after the contents are removed.

Note to Parents

I highly recommend that you hire an appraiser if you own anything of value. Even if you don't think you own much that could be sold for significant value, a professional might be able to find a few treasures. You can expect to pay a professional appraiser between $120 and $200 an hour. In the Northeast or West Coast, it might be higher. (In appendix B, I have listed resources for finding an appraiser as well as a number of organizations you can turn to for information and assistance.)

A Shoulder to Lean On

Having to handle all the details of a funeral and the liquidation of your parents' estate ranks high on the list of stressors that can wreak havoc on a person, so there's another type of help that you will need. This falls in the category of compassionate support. You and your siblings really need a lot of shoulders to lean on during this time. This is the time to make those withdrawals from your emotional bank accounts of close friends. If you are active in a church or synagogue, by all means let your pastor or rabbi know what you're going through and be open to any acts of kindness from your congregation.

Grief can bring with it the symptoms of clinical depression, yet you'll feel as if you have to be the strong one for the sake of your family. It's not a sign of weakness to meet with a counselor and unload what's happening during this stressful time. In fact, with nearly every client, I've found myself holding the hand of an angry, heartbroken, grieving son or daughter. Many of them will be in a very vulnerable state, feeling angry and lashing out because of all the decisions and work they have had to do because their parents did not take care of the issues while they were alive. Then their anger turns to guilt because they realize their parents are no longer here, and they feel guilty because they feel angry. It is a cycle I see often.

You really do have to be strong and think straight as you go through your parents' home for the last time, so take advantage of resources—personal and professional—that can help you cope with the sadness and stress.

Keep in mind, you don't have to go through this alone. There is reliable and trustworthy help that can make this painful experience go smoothly if you just take a little time to look for it. And whatever the financial cost, it will be offset by the relief and value these professionals will provide.

What Do I Do Now?

Current situation: various—some of these things should be done well before your parents decline in health; others need to be done at their passing.

☑ *Begin a list of professionals your parents may need.* Everything from attorneys, financial planners, appraisers, Realtors, and funeral directors.

☑ *Contact your own attorney.* You may need an attorney to assist with the execution of the will.

☑ *Check references.* Before you hire any professional, ask for a list of references, and check at least two.

☑ *Recruit a friend.* Ask a trusted and close friend to be available for you during any periods of a parent's illness or death, even if just to hang out with or be able to call in the middle of the night.

Eleven

How to Clean Out
Your Parents' Estate

You've come a long way, and believe it or not, you're closing in on the finish line. You have a few more important decisions to make when it comes to your parents' estate, and I will do my best to give you some clear-cut options.

At this point in the process, you have already divided up any property you and your siblings wanted or that were covered in the will. What's left is a house full of stuff no one in your family wants. Your first decision is whether to hire a professional or whether you and your siblings will clear things out yourselves. I can't make that decision for you, but here are the things you should consider before deciding:

- Your physical ability to move heavy items

- Your tolerance for this type of work

- Having the time in your schedule to do it

- Your knowledge of local resources and rules/regulations of the community

If you choose to use a professional, it would benefit you greatly to research and choose an expert who provides a total turnkey solution or as close to one as possible. This will greatly minimize the need for you to be personally involved; plus, it will bring you peace of mind. Be mindful that not all professionals will provide a total turnkey or complete solution to the task at hand. You may very well have to use a combination of these resources plus a little physical labor to get it all done.

Your next decision has to do with how to actually dispose of everything left in the house, and again, you have options. Let's look at a few of them.

Estate Sale

Conducting an estate sale is no easy task. Much manpower and organizational skills go into a sale. A good estate sale professional will answer your questions, including whether having an estate sale is the most beneficial for your situation. They will also tell you what they will do and what they will not do.

An estate sale is usually conducted on-site, but not always. It usually involves the organization of all items in the home in common categories—for example, all pottery is on one table, china on another, and so on. The home is organized with the estate company's own tables to create a welcoming and open flow of people into the home. Estate sales are very convenient for the family because most sales are over within a day or two at the most. Usually all items in the estate are individually priced, and only the conducting professional can negotiate those prices. In other words, there is control over what items sell for. Some estate sale professionals also offer a clean-out service, including packing up for donation or an outright purchase of leftovers. Some, but not all, estate sale professionals are also appraisers.

It has been my experience that many of the estate sale professionals I have met are quite savvy and know the values of most residential contents. Be sure to ask questions like:

- How long have you been in business?

- May I have references?

- May I see a copy of your contract?

- What are your fees? Percentage or flat fee?

- What other costs are my responsibility?

- What do you recommend for leftover items?

- Will you leave the house empty?

- Are you insured and bonded?

- Are you affiliated with any professional organizations?

Estate sales are usually conducted for a percentage of the overall dollar value of the sale (usually 25 to 35 percent). Antique and collectible dealers use estate sales as one of their more important wholesale sources. Estate sales typically take one to three days to execute, often with a price reduction offered toward the end. Where the survivors of the deceased cannot agree to the disposition of tangible property, a court may order those goods to be sold in an estate sale with the proceeds to be divided between the survivors. Such a sale and division may also be mandated in the will of the deceased.

Auction

An auction is the process of selling or buying goods by offering them up for bids. The highest bid is the successful buyer. Many feel that an auction is a true indicator of market value. In other words, if the maple desk sells for $100, the market has spoken. The bidding is controlled by the auctioneer, who will do his best to get the bids as high as possible. Some auctioneers are also appraisers, but not all. Like estate sale professionals, they see so much every day and have so much experience with residential contents, many of them are quite savvy.

There are two types of auctions: absolute and reserve. Absolute means it will sell to the highest bidder regardless of what the price may be. If the highest bid is $10, the item sells for $10 regardless of its worth. A reserve auction means the seller can set a minimum price to protect the piece if it doesn't sell for the reserve price. If your reserve price on the highboy is $1,500, and the bidding closes at $1,000, the item will not sell. The seller has the right to accept or reject the highest bid.

That being said, auctions can be a viable way to liquidate a house full of items. I have seen it go both ways. Some bidders are quite enthusiastic and bid very high, and other bidders can be very slow to get started, and the sales price is less than they hoped for. I encourage talking with local auction companies and asking them the same questions listed earlier. An auction company will usually come and pick up the items to be sold, which can be a benefit for the family.

Consignment

Another option is to take the unwanted items to a consignment store. The store keeps between 35 and 50 percent of the money received and gives the rest to you. Sometimes the consignment store will come and pick up from an estate, take it back to the store, price it, and sell it within three to four months, often much sooner. If an item does not sell within a certain time period, the store may lower the price. If the item does not sell at all, you may have the option of retrieving the item, or it can be donated on your behalf to a local charity.

Be sure to ask about fees and time frames. If you do not have a huge amount of leftovers but still have some nice-quality items, such as china, silver, framed prints, decorative items, and so on, consignment might be a good choice for you.

Donation

There are times when families have requested donating the entire remainder of the estate to a worthy charity. This process is simple, easy, and comes with a tax receipt. I usually provide my clients who request this service with an itemization of all items that have been boxed and bagged.

If most of what is left over looks to be donation items, such as older appliances, linens, kitchenware, clothing, bedding, and so on, then donation is probably the best option for you. All items should be neatly boxed up, so the charity can pick up all the items in a timely fashion with their hand trucks.

Be sure to call them two to three weeks in advance, and call them again once or twice to reconfirm your appointment and address.

Clearing Out the House

If you've put into practice everything I've advised thus far, you've really gotten the hardest work behind you. The emotional and mental strain that goes with settling your parents' affairs is done, and all that's left is rolling up your sleeves and tackling the stuff. Not that it will be easy handling all the things your parents owned that will bring up wonderful memories, but there's something about backbreaking, sweat-inducing labor that keeps the emotions at bay. Based on my experience clearing out more than three hundred homes, you are a few days away from being finished with the last difficult phase of clearing out the family home.

In the next few pages, I will explain my proven techniques on how you can accomplish the job of physically clearing out a house. There is a method to the madness. As a bonus, these techniques will help you if you ever decide to downsize your own home, something most of us boomers should seriously consider. (For more on how to downsize your home, see chapter 13.) By the end of this "Oh, my aching back" task at hand, you may not want any more stuff to lug back to your house. Clearing out a home produces an effect much like that of aversion therapy. Once you see all the accumulation out in the open, you do not want any more of it at your house.

As with any task, if you have the right system for clearing out your parents' house, the process will go much more smoothly. Here's a little preparation.

First, remove from the house any and all property that has been divided among the heirs. Make sure everyone has removed all that they were granted. This will offer more room for you to work in the home.

Second, have all valuables or perceived valuables already identified. What should be remaining in the home are leftovers from what the heirs did not want, either for an estate sale or auction, or to be packed up for donation or consignment. If the heirs do not want the valuables, or there are no heirs, an estate sale professional will liquidate the contents and may clear out the home for you at an additional cost.

Third, consult with an estate professional to see what you should clean out. Some liquidators will handpick what should go into the sale and pack up the rest for donation, but you may want to go through everything first.

If you are cleaning out the house yourself, do not proceed until these three things have been done.

The Do-It-Yourself Clean Out

If you have made the decision to clean out your parents' house by yourself, here are my tried-and-true strategies for getting it done in a timely manner. As I have mentioned, if you follow the process outlined in this book, you can clean out your parents' estate in ten days or less.

Regardless of how neat and tidy your parents may have been, this will be a dirty job, so dress accordingly. This is jeans-and-a-long-sleeved-shirt kind of work, and even if you're doing this in the warmer months, don't wear shorts. Also, a good pair of gloves is a must, and you should also have a supply of disposable latex gloves. For protection in dusty attics and dank basements, wear some type of mask over your mouth—you'll find them in the paint section of your local hardware or building supply store. While you're there, pick up a pair of knee pads and Velcro back support because in most attics, you'll either be on your hands and knees or bent and twisting at the waist for hours.

To further tend to your backs, rent a good hand truck from a local rental agency—the type with a strap to keep larger items in place as you move them. Also, it's a good idea to bring a wheelbarrow to cart the large trash bags to the curb. Bring along a toolbox or at least a couple of screwdrivers, a pair of pliers, a measuring tape, and a hammer. There's a pretty good chance you'll need to remove at least one door from its hinges to squeeze some of the larger items out.

Speaking of workers, if you have some college- or high school-aged young men in the family, draft them into service, especially if you or your siblings have any health issues such as back problems or arthritis. I'm in reasonably good shape for a boomer, and my assistant is a tough woman herself, but the wear and tear on our bodies takes its toll. Most of what is involved at this stage is bending, kneeling, lifting, and climbing. Occasionally we become contortionists, but only momentarily. Let the teenagers do the heavy lifting. If you don't have any teenagers or they can't get away from college or work, consider hiring a couple of younger people to help you. If there's a college nearby, their student services office usually has a list of students available for day or weekend work. If there is no college nearby, consider contacting your local Boy Scouts or church youth groups.

Other supplies you will need are at least six rolls of packing tape, approximately thirty to fifty boxes, and a box of one hundred heavy-duty black garbage bags. Don't get the wimpy ones!

Since you'll be discarding a lot of stuff, this raises another issue: what do you do with all those bags when you're done? Believe it or not, in about 20 percent of the estates I've liquidated, I need to rent a Dumpster to handle all the garbage. You may not need one, but you should at least call your local county waste removal service to let them know what you're doing and that you may have a very large pile of garbage bags on the curb. In some counties, you must request a bulk pickup, and other counties will only allow a certain number of trash bags. Since most communities don't like to have those piles lying around very long (raccoons and other pests love to make a mess), be courteous to the neighbors, and arrange a special pickup. This may mean hiring an outside debris removal company to haul it away if the county is not set up to assist you.

You should also contact a local recycling center—either a commercial business or a city-sponsored program—and a nonprofit such as the Kidney Foundation or a local crisis shelter. I'm a big fan of keeping as much stuff out of landfills as possible, and much of what you plan to throw away can be either recycled or donated to those less fortunate. It might sound like a lot of work, but these few phone calls will lighten your work load considerably.

This is a good place to discuss paper. Believe it or not, paper could actually account for the bulk of the weight you have to move. The record in all of my estate *clean outs* is thirty-nine thousand pounds of paper! True, that was several thousand pounds more than the typical estate, but it gives you an idea of how much paper you could run into. For some reason, our parents kept just about every piece of paper, magazine, and newspaper that ever entered their homes. The members of this generation were great letter writers, and I have run across hundreds of boxes of old letters. You'll also find tax records going back to the Depression and a lifetime of bank statements, junk mail, receipts, coupons, catalogs, and recipes.

Aside from the letters of days gone by that may add value to your family stories, virtually none of this is worth keeping, but don't just throw it in the Dumpster. Much of this paper contains information in demand by identity thieves who cruise neighborhoods looking for large stashes of refuse. They will go through all those bags, looking to steal anything with a Social Security number or bank account information. Inside homes that children have started cleaning out, we find many trash bags that are full of bank statements, other financial papers, and even checkbooks of a recently deceased parent. This is not good! These items need to be destroyed in an appropriate manner such as shredding. Most cities have businesses such as Shred-It or Automated Shredding Service, which will come to your location with industrial-strength paper shredders to shred all of your paper. Unless you have a surefire way of disposing the paper so that no one can use it for illicit purposes, hire a commercial shredding firm to handle it for you. It's better to have peace of mind.

Finally, prepare in advance to make sure everyone has plenty of water or soft drinks available, and arrange for any meals you will need. They say an army travels on its stomach, and your army of workers will stay a lot happier if they're not hungry and can take a break now and then to rehydrate and munch on a granola bar.

Supplies You'll Need

- A can-do attitude
- Work clothes—jeans and a long-sleeved shirt
- Leather gloves and latex gloves

- Respirator or dust masks
- Kneepads and back support
- Hand truck
- Wheelbarrow
- Toolbox: screwdrivers (flat and Phillips), pliers, measuring tape, hammer
- Bug spray
- Insect bombs for attic and basement—use one week prior to going in
- At least six rolls of packing tape
- Permanent markers for labeling boxes
- Box of one hundred heavy-duty black garbage bags
- Thirty to fifty boxes (may be more or less, depending on the estate)

Survey the Scene

Now that you're prepared for a long day of hard work, take a few minutes to see what you're up against. I always start with a walk-through, checking every room, the attic, basement, garage, and any storage sheds. I open every cabinet and drawer, peek under beds, and brave every closet (do your best to keep a poker face), making mental notes of where the trouble spots are. By trouble spots, I mean the places with the stuff that causes you to gasp, "Oh my!" This should also give you a good idea of how much of the contents you will recycle, donate, or discard.

Make sure you have a notepad with you to write down specific challenges for every room. For example, perhaps your parents have a huge piano that you cannot move or lift. Obviously a professional mover must be hired for this kind of special challenge. Or you might find a basement full of chemicals, paints, and other hazardous material you don't even recognize. For that scenario, you may need to hire a hauling company to properly dispose of these at a chemical dump site. Maybe you helped your dad assemble a desk for his den, and it's too big to get through the door. Assign someone to disassemble it while the others are clearing out other rooms. Another family had a huge aquarium that required some expertise in draining it and transferring the exotic tropical fish to another location. Note any of these types of special cases and develop a plan for handling them.

A couple of things I look for during the walk-through are two rooms that can be dedicated to collecting certain items. One room we call the *safe room*. This room is used as a temporary home for anything of value that may be found and will be given to family later or sold at the estate sale, but its fate is not yet decided. Usually a bedroom will work. The next room is the *donation room*. This one needs to be the largest room possible because more will be donated than you realize: clothing, pots, pans, and kitchen utensils, linens, clothes, and so on.

Once you get into the actual moving process, start an assembly line by instructing your volunteers to take appropriate items to these two rooms. This will bring some order to the process and allow you to make any last-minute decisions about where things eventually end up. The rest of the home can be used to place items that will go to the estate sale, auction, or consignment.

As you go through the house, make notes of any safety issues. For example, the attic is a prime opportunity for injury. Most attics do not have floors, only a few planks or boards laid across the rafters. One slip, and someone's leg or body could go through the ceiling below. If there's a lot of work to be done in the attic, you may need to bring in some additional boards to create a secure pathway to the contents you need to remove. Also, if there's no lighting, bring along a couple of shop lights to hang from the ceiling. If access to the attic does not include a pull-down ladder or stairway, bring along a sturdy ladder for the job. And bring a can of insect spray or set off a bug bomb a week ahead of time because most attics will have wasps, hornets, bees, and spiders that can make working up there unpleasant. If you suspect rodents such as mice or rats are in the attic, arrange to have a professional exterminator come to the house at least several days prior to cleaning. I've even run into nonpoisonous snakes in attics.

Speaking of attics, this area generally presents the hardest work with the least rewards. I've discovered that our parents' generation used the attic to store things they should have thrown away long ago. In every estate I've liquidated, 90 percent of the attic contents are thrown out with a small percentage to be donated. You're going to find a lot of empty cardboard boxes—maybe all the boxes your parents used when they moved into the home will be stored in the attic (just in case they move again, I guess). You're also going to find a lot of boxes of old textbooks—theirs as well as the ones you used when you were in grammar school. Here's also where old newspapers and magazines end up, broken lamps, long-forgotten clothing, stereos, odd furniture, and piles of stuff that has lost its usability. Attics are very interesting to clean out. You never know what you're going to find.

Older homes are notorious for rickety stairways leading down into the basement. They were probably just barely adequate for your mom and dad to use, but if a couple of guys are trying to carry a chest freezer up those stairs, the stairs may need some reinforcing, or the guys need to use another door if possible. Many counties will only haul away an appliance if the door is removed to prevent anyone such as a small child from getting stuck inside. Some will allow duct tape around the circumference of the piece, but call and ask your local waste removal company. Remove all throw rugs and runners to prevent tripping. Unplug the television and other electronic devices, and roll up the usual rat's nest of extension cords so no one trips.

If possible, only one person should do the walk-through, and that should be the designated team leader of the estate. Trust me, trying to do this as a group project will slow things down and open up possibilities for disputes. Remember, the purpose of the walk-through is not to make hard-and-fast decisions but to get the lay of the land, so to speak. I recommend doing the walk-through at least two to three weeks prior to the estate sale or auction.

Getting Started

Never attempt to clear out a house alone. Work in teams—involve several family members if you can. There's strength in numbers, plus it's just a good way to turn a hard job into some fun.

Once the appointed hour has come and everyone has arrived, consider beginning with one of the icebreakers I suggested in chapter 8. Remember, even though this is hard work, it's one of the last opportunities for you and your siblings to celebrate your parents. You'd be amazed how it sets the tone if your family arrives to the smell of fresh coffee and sees a plate of doughnuts, fresh fruit, or granola bars on the counter. Take a little extra time to create a pleasant atmosphere, and things will get off to a great start.

When it's time to go to work, explain the concept of the safe room and donation room, and let everyone know which rooms you've selected for those purposes. Talk about working together as a team, two people to a room, working side by side. One pulls things out; the other packs it up or runs it to one of the two designated rooms. It's like a team of horses—what would happen if they all went in different directions? Nothing would get accomplished. But if you all pull together, it can work. Be sure to limit the number of people in the house at any given time to six people. If you have more than six people who want to be involved in the cleaning process, then arrange to work in shifts. When there are more than six people in the home, then everyone starts getting confused as to what goes where, and in which room. That kind of situation can lead to bickering, nitpicking, and even stealing. In my experience, the easiest and most efficient way to clean a home is to choose six people to work at least four-hour shifts. Then you can begin making assignments.

One word of caution here: as a team leader, you're sort of the foreman on the job. Be careful not to bark out orders while not doing any of the work yourself because resentment will soon follow. Even though I'm the Estate Lady, I go in up to my elbows just like everyone else, and you should too. Everyone does his fair share when it comes to cleaning out the house.

The Attic

When clearing out a house, I recommend starting from the top and working your way down. So the attic and upper floor, if it's a multistory house, go first. These usually involve the most work, so as you work your way down, the day will seem to go easier. Since the attic is usually the dirtiest job of all, I suggest you assign that to yourself and two other people to hand things down, so you don't have to keep climbing up and down a rickety ladder. One person should be in the attic, one on the ladder, and one running the item to a designated room. (Sometimes an attic will have a strategically placed window to throw things out of into a Dumpster below.)

Most of what is found in an attic will be discarded to the curb or sent to donation. Two words of caution, though: use your eyes and hands to search the nooks and crannies of the rafters. We have found pieces of jewelry tucked away up there, so leave no stone unturned. If you see an obvious loose floorboard, look under it because you never know if that's where Dad hid his gold coins. (Remember, your parents' generation tended to hide their valuables out of mistrust of banks, so be very careful as you go through their items. I'll give you a few tips about this treasure hunting at the end of the chapter.)

Make sure you are in long jeans and long sleeves, wearing a dust mask and back support. Also make sure the attic was bombed for insects prior to your working up there. Getting bitten by a poisonous spider is not a pleasant experience. While three people are up near the attic, commencing the clean out, offer each of your other siblings or helpers a room to work in. I will give tips on where they should begin shortly.

Special Challenges

Use your notes from the walk-through to point out any special challenges, and remind everyone that if they run into a situation where they just don't know what to do, call a time-out and get everyone's input. For example, someone may be disassembling a bed, and as they remove the mattress, they discover an envelope of hundred-dollar bills or maybe a handgun. (If a gun is found, do not handle it. Go and get someone who is knowledgeable in checking to see if it is loaded. Many times, hidden weapons are loaded, which is why I suggest leaving it untouched for the time being.) No one knew about this hidden treasure, there was no mention of it in the will, and it has potential value.

By this time, I hope you and your siblings have established an atmosphere of trust and cooperation, so no one is going to try to sneak it out to his car. In a case like this, you set the items aside in the safe room. When the house is cleared out, you divide these unknown valuables fairly, using the principle of financial equity (if it's money, everyone gets an equal portion; if it's a valuable, you either sell it or allow someone to keep it by paying its fair value and dividing the proceeds with the other siblings).

We're almost ready for the hard work to begin, but first, remind everyone that if anything of monetary value or sentimental value is found, it will be set aside to sell, and if they want any of those items, they will have a chance later to either buy them or divide them so that everyone receives an equal amount of value. This exercise is just for those things that have little or no monetary value but may be special to them. Try to encourage them to be selective and not take too much stuff because the division of property has already taken place, but don't make too much of a big deal over this. If your sister wants to fill her car with mementos, let her. But gently remind her that one day her son or daughter will have to do this kind of work when she's gone.

Now it's time to turn up the hi-fi and get started!

Who to Call

- Local waste removal company to ask how they can help you
- Debris or rubbish-hauling company
- Charities that accept and pick up donations (call two to three weeks in advance, and reconfirm the specific date and time)
- County or municipal recycling center
- Professional shredding company (for important personal, medical, or financial documents that the executor no longer needs or that could be used in identity theft)

Helpful Hints

You walk into the room that's assigned to you, ready to clear everything out and get this ordeal behind you. You're upbeat and optimistic, knowing that in a few hours you and your siblings will have accomplished a huge task. And then you open a closet and see all the clutter, and your heart sinks. *How am I ever going to get just this one room cleared out?* you think. While emptying a house isn't rocket science, I've learned that an orderly process makes the job easier.

Before you begin, make sure you have the necessary supplies (see "Supplies You'll Need" on pages 154–55), including plenty of boxes and permanent markers. Remember, after packing and sealing each box, list the contents of that box either on the box itself or in a separate list. That way, you can keep track of the contents of each box and locate items when you need them later.

Clothing and linens. Arrange for two people in each room to work as an assembly line, starting with all clothing and linens throughout the house. This includes clothing, blankets, towels, washcloths—anything made out of cloth. Have every helper in every bedroom begin by packing the clothing, shoes, and linens. First, there's usually a lot of it, and second, it's relatively easy to move. Also, surviving family members generally do not want to keep any of it. For some reason, very few see any sentimental value in their parents' clothing. If it's in good shape and usable, the best thing to do with used clothing and linens is to donate them to a homeless shelter, charity, or resale shop. I wouldn't even bother to try to sell it because that will just take extra time, and you won't get much for it anyway. (Top-of-the-line designer clothing, fur coats, or leather jackets might be exceptions.) If you're tempted to keep any of it, try to imagine a poor person in the winter or someone down on his luck who might need a suit for a job interview. Box it up neatly, and place all these boxes in the donation room. Ideally, a shelter or charity of your choice will send a truck to the home, where they can just load it up and take it away. In a very short period of time, every clothes closet and dresser drawer and linen closet will be empty.

Bathrooms. The next thing to tackle is the bathrooms. Clear off all counters and under the sink, finish emptying the linen closet, and dispose of personal toiletries, medicine, first aid items, old heating pads, and ice packs. Since none of this has much value, just bag it up and dispose of it. Do not allow the big, black bags to just sit there and trip someone; remove them from the home, and take them to the curb two at a time.

Clearing out the bathrooms is a little secret we discovered quite by accident. Even though they are generally small, you can stack a lot of donation boxes in the bathtub or shower if you have to for added space. As you find chemicals and cleaning supplies, place them in separate boxes or buckets from the garage. These should not go to the landfill. If you do not want these supplies, ask the neighbors if they want them. Or if there is an abundance, have someone pick them up and take them to the chemical dump site for you. There are very few decisions that need to be made with closets and bathrooms. Just clean them out, and dispose of or donate the items unless you find a hidden treasure that should be placed in the safe room.

After the closets and bathrooms, go after the knickknacks—all that stuff on the tops of dressers, end tables, and shelves. Figurines, brushes and combs, bowls filled with coins, matchbooks, golf tees, nail files, and the like. Make sure at all times that you have at least three boxes and one roll of tape near you. Place all of these knickknacks in the box, and put it in the donation room or in the area, like the living room, where you are collecting items you feel confident will sell at an estate sale.

Spare bedrooms. Spare bedrooms are also often used by older people as an extension of the attic, so don't be surprised to find stacks of magazines, newspapers, old containers, and empty boxes. When the attic got too full or it was too hard for your parents to climb, a spare bedroom became the catchall.

What should be left in that room now is furniture and stuff no one in the family usually wants. Time to grab a heavy-duty trash bag to clear out everything that needs to be discarded. If it is mostly paper, remember to recycle as much as you can. (Don't forget to label your bags of personal papers so they go to the shredder.) Then it's time for the bigger stuff, and here's where you will have options. If ahead of time you have determined there are enough salable items to warrant an estate sale, leave the furniture right where it is and tag it "to be sold." On the day of the sale, customers will want to inspect the furniture, so don't disassemble it or move it. The estate sale professional will do that. If the home will be the site of an estate sale or auction, save yourself some extra work by leaving heavy pieces right where they are.

All the while this is going on, there are three team members upstairs, emptying the attic. This means that the top floor of the house or hallway of a ranch-style home is now completely filled with stuff. At this point, everyone should take a break, rehydrate and eat, and then pitch in to get rid of the stuff that came down from the attic. Most of it will be bagged up and carried to the curb. One of the attic workers should have been bringing things to designated rooms while all the other activity was going on in the house. Once the stuff is cleared, everyone moves forward with their new assignment.

Fast Facts

Some interesting statistics based on my experience:

- Homes needing a Dumpster: roughly 20 percent (if you recycle cardboard and paper, the need will be greatly diminished)

- Overall contents thrown away: 20 to 25 percent (in cases of hoarding it is significantly increased)

- Overall contents that are donated: 50 to 80 percent

- Overall contents suitable for an estate sale: approximately 30 to 35 percent

Bedrooms. Moving from top to bottom, the bedrooms usually come next. Since the closets were the first to be emptied, these can be used to temporarily get things out of the way while you strip the bedrooms. Disassemble each bed, and place the headboard, mattress, and box springs on their sides against a long wall. This should allow more space to move. Move all smaller furniture closer together, like the nightstands and lamps. Box up any remaining items in each bedroom.

Kitchen and pantry. Often, the kitchen is one of the more challenging rooms in the house. Do not be fooled! Even the smallest of kitchens can seem to defy the laws of physics by having lots of items in a small space. The best way to handle the kitchen is with the fewest number of people possible, to avoid tripping hazards and to allow enough elbow room in which to work. I suggest that you choose two people to take care of all the packing in the kitchen. (Keep in mind that the fewer people in this room, the faster it will get done.)

First, the two people can box up any canned goods or food items that are still within the expiration date. Label each box to take to the local soup kitchen, church, or shelter. Some organizations will even come get it. Any and all perishables and expired food need to be thrown out immediately. It's not worth leaving it up to chance should someone take ill from bad food.

Next, the same two people will handle all the glassware. You will find dozens of glasses, some that match and some that don't. On average, the kitchens I've worked in contain anywhere from forty-five to ninety drinking glasses: highball glasses, martini glasses, iced-tea glasses, on-the-rocks glasses, wineglasses, water goblets, cordial glasses, and mason jars, just for starters. If you or your siblings have a summer cabin or you have children in college or starting out in their first apartments, you may have some use for this stuff. But most of these, with one exception, end up in the donation room. If your mother had a collection of fine china, crystal, or silver, it may be worthwhile putting it in a sale.

In the kitchen cabinets, you will find Tupperware and acrylic items as well. If your plan is to conduct an estate sale, leave all the crystal and better glassware. Matching sets are best. All others, including plastic, can be boxed up and donated. Please discard used Tupperware, and recycle other containers such as the infamous Cool Whip containers, baby jars, and sour cream and margarine containers. You will likely find an abundance of these.

Countertop appliances, such as coffee makers, electric can openers, mixers, and microwaves, are perfect for estate sales if they are not too old. If they have some age on them but still work, off they go to the donation room. That leaves us with pots and pans, cooking utensils, everyday china, flatware, and drawers filled with about anything.

Box up the pots and pans for donation, and discard what you find in most of the drawers. You will find coupons, recipes, addresses, letters, scrap paper and notepads, clothes pins, paper clips, rubber bands, bread twister ties (my personal favorite), oodles of plastic grocery bags, newspaper clippings, milk bottle caps, and many other things. You name it, it's in there! Unless there is something you would like to have, let it all go.

China, dinnerware, and flatware can all be sold at a sale along with ice buckets, cookie jars, and decanter sets.

After you've gone through the kitchen, congratulate yourself, and don't forget to take a break now and then. Keep drinks and munchies available, and enjoy yourselves because there's still a lot of work to do.

Content Categories

As you survey your parents' home, the contents should be divided into the following categories:

- *Sentimental value.* Anything that carries a poignant memory of your parents that you would like to keep. This could include old photographs, a wedding ring, your dad's favorite fishing pole or your mom's hand mirror. Warning: be careful not to view everything as having sentimental value.

- *Monetary value.* Items that could be sold for significant sums of money. To get an accurate value of these items, hire a professional appraiser. These items may be divided among family members (always seeking financial equity) or sold, with the proceeds divided equally among the siblings.

- *Donations.* Any item in good condition that could be used by someone else. This usually includes clothing, furniture, dishes and other kitchen equipment, appliances, and so on. Agencies such as the Kidney Foundation and Salvation Army will pick up these if you have a sufficient quantity.

- *Recyclables.* Between 50 and 75 percent of everything removed from a home should not go to the landfill. Contact a local shredding company to come to the house and shred all paper. Plastic, glass, old lumber, and old car batteries should be recycled.

- *Hazardous materials.* Contact a local refuse company or the municipal environmental office for assistance in removing hazardous materials such as old paint cans, paint thinner, pesticides and herbicides, cleaning supplies, and antifreeze. The garages of older homes often have large quantities of environmentally harmful material.

- *Trash.* Approximately 20 to 25 percent of the items in a typical estate liquidation will be thrown away. Contact a local refuse company to arrange a bulk pickup so the trash will not be left too long at the curb. In some cases, you may need to rent a Dumpster to contain all the trash.

Once you've cleared out the attic, bedrooms, bathrooms, and kitchen, the main-floor rooms, such as the living room, dining room, and den, are next. You may have filled those rooms already with things to be donated and things to save for selling or dividing with your family, so you might need to fill up a truck and make a run to the local charity or recycle place to free up some space. (Charities will often come to you if you have enough space to stack donation items. If not, you may have to haul a few things to them to clear out some space.) Hopefully, you have taken my suggestion to bring all trash bags out to the curb as you fill them, two at a time, or to a Dumpster so you don't have a huge pile to contend with at once. In other words, reorganize a bit so you have room for the rest of the job.

If you're planning on having an estate sale, you may be able to leave most of the furniture and other main-floor items for sale in place. However, most of the furniture I see in the average home is an outdated style and really not worth trying to sell. It's usually 1970s style, and even if it's in great condition, it will not bring a decent price to justify an estate sale. An appraiser can help you decide, but most dated furniture from the '70s, '80s, and '90s ends up being donated.

Follow the same process on the lower level that you did when you were upstairs. You'll be surprised how much stuff for the Dumpster lurks in corners, behind furniture, and in closets, so keep those trash bags handy. You might also be surprised at what you find hidden away on the main floor. In one house, we found seventy-six half-empty bottles of liquor, and, no, we didn't have a big party after we were finished. We poured it all down the sink, and the house smelled like a college dorm party.

After the main floor is cleared, all that's left is the basement, garage, and outbuilding or tool shed. Often these areas can hold a lot of stuff, and most of it is hardly worth saving. Because most basements are damp, there's a good chance any clothing will be mildewed and either need to be cleaned or thrown away. Basements are also where Dad kept his tools, fishing and hunting equipment, and other things related to his hobbies. Some of these items might be in good enough condition to sell but might be rusted and water stained beyond use. As with the attic, an assembly-line approach with a couple of helpers working the stairs will expedite the process. If there's a freezer in the basement or garage, you'll need to decide what to do with the food. But unless you know how long the food has been in the freezer, get rid of it.

Garages will either be relatively clear or piled to the ceiling; for some reason, there's no middle ground with garages. And when they're full of boxes and piles, it's usually with the kinds of things that go straight to the throwaway pile. The nicest thing I can say about the garage is that it's on ground level with a big door to back a truck up to.

One word of caution when it comes to the garage: this is where you'll find the largest supply of toxic and environmentally unfriendly material: half-empty paint cans, gasoline, kerosene, and motor oil. All sorts of solvents, such as paint thinners and turpentine as well as poisonous products meant to kill weeds, bugs, and other critters will also be there. Handle this material carefully by wearing gloves, and check with local refuse haulers or environmental agencies for the safest way to dispose of this material. Lawn equipment, snow blowers, power tools, and other larger items may be sold or divided among the family.

Treasure Hunting and Other Surprises

Although I have cautioned you not to spend too much time handling every item in your parents' home, I need to offer one word of caution that will probably slow you down. When it comes to clearing out every room, closet, and corner of the house, be thorough, and anticipate some hidden valuables. Many older people had a long-term distrust of banks and often hid valuables in the strangest places. If your parents were European immigrants, they will have an even greater tendency to do this, and if either of your parents had dementia or Alzheimer's, they likely hid things and forgot about them. So you'll all need to use some detective skills to make sure you aren't leaving anything valuable behind.

As I mentioned earlier, I've found diamond jewelry hidden in velvet Crown Royal bags and stuffed between the rafters in an attic. Three good places to check for treasures are toilet tanks, ice cube trays, and canister sets. I've also found valuables hidden in microwaves and rolled up in pantyhose in a dresser drawer. I've made it a practice to squeeze every rolled-up pair of socks or folded underwear because I've found jewelry in them. One time when we were cleaning out a kitchen, we started pouring the sugar from the canister into the sink. Thinking about this, we grabbed a strainer, and started pouring the contents of the sugar canister through it. Then the coffee. Sure enough, when I got to the flour, a diamond ring landed in the strainer. A *big* diamond ring that could have easily ended up in the trash!

Places to Find Hidden Treasures

Many seniors hide money and valuables that often go unnoticed in the liquidation of their estates. Here are the most common methods or places where these valuables may exist:

Clothing and shoes—especially breast pockets in a man's suit coat, under an insert in the sole of a shoe, wrapped in socks or underwear, bra cups

Drapery hems—a favorite hiding place for small jewelry or coins

Canister sets—rare coins or jewelry in the flour or sugar canister and sometimes cookie tins

Books—paper money slid between the pages of a book

Ice cube trays—a favorite place for small jewelry or gemstones

Toilet tank—another place for jewelry

Duct tape—money or jewelry wrapped tightly in a wadded ball

Picture frames—between the picture and the mat or backing material

Attic rafters—favorite place for coins, jewelry, and antiques

Here's another clue from Detective Hall. If you find any crumpled-up wads of duct tape, open them up. It'll take you a while, but do it because I've found expensive pieces of jewelry in them. Along the same lines, assign one of the youngsters to go through every book in the house, flipping through the pages to see what drops out. We've found thousands of dollars hidden in books over the years. Another place where I've found hidden money is in shoes, but don't just peek inside and think you've come up empty. A lot of elderly people used those inserts in the soles. If you see those in a pair of shoes, peel them back because that's where I've found gold coins and folded twenty-dollar bills. Instruct everyone to go through clothing pockets, look inside vases and shake them, check between pictures and the backing material of the frame, and peel back the plastic lids of old coffee cans.

Most people are amazed that I can think like the older generation can, especially if dementia or Alzheimer's is part of the equation. But I try to put myself in the shoes of an older person who has a few valuable things and is fearful of having them stolen or paranoid something will happen to them. You can see signs in the home that they really tried hard to think of places to hide things to protect them. Most of the time, though, they forget, and the kids never know where to find them. Sometimes I imagine being on a limited, fixed income and worried that I'll someday need extra money. So where would I hide it? These fears are very real to our dear parents and grandparents, but the sad thing is that they usually forget about them, and the children may jump to the conclusion that these items have been stolen or given away. That might very well be the case, too, but it is possible that they are just well hidden.

As you go through the process of clearing out your parents' home, I hope you will experience a little bonus benefit. It may include a little anger because of all the emotions that accompany this process; anger and resentment are often predominant. They usually hit when you're right in the middle of the most cluttered room or as you carry bag after bag of junk to the curb: "Mom, why did you collect all this stuff? What were you thinking? And why did you leave it all for us to clean up!"

It's okay to feel this way. But please recognize the benefit in this situation is that you will begin to look at your own collecting habits and determine to downsize in the near future. When you stop and think of it, we regularly use about 20 percent of what we own. The other 80 percent that we don't use is just sitting in our closets, garages, and attics. You might own twenty pairs of shoes, but I'll bet you regularly wear only three or four of them. You've got forty blouses, but only eight or nine of them make the daily rotation, right? I'm encouraged by the trend of a lot of boomers to sell their big houses and move into condominiums. Boomers call me and tell me they want to simplify their lives and homes. I think they're realizing that life (or happiness) isn't about things and owning the biggest house on the block. They are beginning to feel that life is a blur these days, and they prefer to have an easier lifestyle.

As you carry all those bags of stuff to the curb in front of your parents' home, begin a mental walk-through of your own home. Then make yourself this promise: *for one month, I'm going to add one extra bag to my weekly trash pickup and take at least one box to a donation center.* Why just one month? They say if you do something for thirty days, it becomes a habit, and this is one addiction that will be good for you and your family and benefit others as well.

What Do I Do Now?

Current situation: shortly before and on the day of the estate liquidation.

☑ *Get the right equipment.* Make sure you have the right tools, a hand truck, protective clothing, heavy-duty trash bags, and anything else you may need when everyone arrives to clear out the house.

☑ *Contact refuse and recycling companies.* If there is an inordinate amount of throwaway items, you may need to rent a Dumpster.

☑ *Inform your parents' neighbors.* As a courtesy, let them know there will be a lot of activity next door and that you have notified the refuse company to make a special pickup of the pile of trash bags at the curb.

☑ *Order pizza.* Make arrangements for food and refreshments for everyone helping.

Twelve

Right, Wrong, and In Between

Sam was only forty years old when he died. When the family contacted me to liquidate his estate, I learned that he served in the technology industry, was divorced with three children, and lived as a bachelor in a very nice home with lovely furnishings. Sam loved music and theater and had an impressive collection of musical instruments. He entertained frequently, grilling on a well-appointed patio or inviting friends over for drinks. He also loved the holidays—he owned more Christmas decorations than four families put together! In short, except for the divorce, which is fairly common, he seemed to have the perfect life, which was why I was so surprised to learn how he died: Sam had taken his own life.

This was my first job involving a suicide, and I was surprised at how I reacted emotionally. I always find myself sharing some of the family's grief when I assist them in clearing out their parents' homes, but this time I was often moved to tears as I handled various items during the estate sale preparation. What caused so much suffering for this dear man who owned the contemporary vase I held in my hand? What caused him to lose hope surrounded by so much beauty? I soon discovered the answer and quite by accident.

As I looked in a closet, I found a grocery bag tucked behind the vacuum cleaner. When I opened it, I found stacks of letters and cards addressed to him. They were in no particular order and included many greeting cards with no envelopes. They looked romantic in nature, much like the ones my husband and I exchange. I glanced down, and all I saw were "I love you" and "Yours forever, Sam." Every one of the cards was signed by him. She must have returned them to him at some point, I realized. But there was one card sticking out at the top that almost beckoned me to read it, and it gave me chill bumps. It said, in Sam's handwriting, "I could never live without you. If I have to live without you, I refuse to live." Alone with my sorrow and Sam's thoughts in a closet that belonged to him, I now faced a dilemma.

Do I just dispose of the letters, assuming these cards were never supposed to be found and sparing his family further anguish? Or do I go to the family in the interest of helping them find closure to Sam's tragic death? I chose the latter, feeling I had done the right thing in a difficult situation. It is not my place to dispose of anything of that nature unless I have permission from a family member to do so.

Inside every estate are secrets waiting to come to light. They may be temporarily buried, but they are in there. Most estate situations bring at least one ethical question to resolve. Ethics is all about right and wrong, and you may face several ethical issues as you prepare for and then work through your parents' estate. Some of the answers will not be easy to decipher. There is much gray area when you start walking through your parents' past.

Decisions regarding moving your parents out of their home and into some form of safer, assisted living present one of the biggest ethical challenges, and you will soon discover that the line between right and wrong can become pretty fuzzy. Remember the story of Steve and Debbie from chapter 4? They knew Debbie's parents could no longer live in their family home but couldn't convince them to move. So they took Debbie's parents for a ride in the country, eventually arriving at a wonderful senior housing complex where they escorted their surprised parents into a lovely apartment. This technique worked for them—pushing the issue convinced their parents it was the best place for them to live—but was it right? I have since learned that this practice is not uncommon, but it could also result in bad feelings and even legal challenges.

From a distance, these types of ethical questions might seem easy, but when you are in the middle of it, everything becomes a challenge. I have recently learned of another family facing an almost identical situation, and they, too, moved their parents in a similar manner. Only in this case, one of the parents went into a deep depression for several weeks, longing to return to her home. The family knew the parents were better off in the assisted-living center, but to this day family members feel guilty about what they did.

Of course, the best way to deal with this ethical issue starts before it happens. It's part of that important conversation you need to have when your parents are mentally alert and capable of making sound decisions about what to do if they become physically unable to live in their current home. If that didn't happen and the need for them to move is urgent, always put their safety ahead of any other concerns.

Note to Parents

It may alarm you to think of your children moving you against your will, but you and your spouse could be in danger if you stay in your home when you are beset by physical infirmities. You can protect your children from having to make the decision to move you by either giving explicit instructions for what you want done should you become unable to make the decision or by assigning one of your children power of healthcare attorney. Be assured that children usually do not enjoy doing anything against their parents' wishes.

Family Secrets

Sometimes, clearing out a family home will uncover things you never knew about a parent. I recall one home I was called to clear out, and we found written evidence that the father had had an affair way back in the '40s. This sort of information should be handled with kid gloves. The best advice here is to dispose of any such thing while you are alive that may cause great pain to loved ones if they should find it after you're gone . . . because someone will find it.

In another case, a distraught family called me when their thirty-seven-year-old sister died suddenly from cardiac arrest. Single, Tina lived alone and kept pretty much to herself, but as far as anyone knew, she had no serious health problems. Within the first hour in the home, I had a strong feeling why she died so young. The kitchen was completely void of any type of food with the exception of two six-packs of Diet Coke and two boxes of granola bars. In an otherwise empty cupboard, I found two boxes of crackers. A mouse couldn't have survived on that. Then when I went into the bedroom, I found evidence of an eating disorder. My heart just sank. Poor Tina had literally starved herself to death, convinced she was too fat. Was not telling the family the right thing to do here? Should I mention this to the family or keep it to myself?

With Tina's case, I did not mention my suspicion of an eating disorder to her family, and here's why. First, I expected the family would seek an autopsy since Tina died so young and apparently in otherwise good health. Second, I was fairly certain a physician would notice her thin and frail frame and would mention it in the death report once they had the facts. Third, I knew her brothers and sisters had been in the home for a couple of days prior to my arrival and saw firsthand that there was no food in the house. You may think I did the wrong thing, but these two examples underscore the dilemma you may face with family secrets. Access to information like this places an enormous power in your hands to heal or hurt. The last thing I would ever want to do is add to anyone's pain.

As you walk through your deceased parents' home, you may find evidence that one of your parents had an illicit relationship, a secret habit, a stash of illegal weapons, or pornographic material. You may discover that your father hadn't filed tax returns for several years or that your mom had given a child up for adoption when she was seventeen. In other words, you may discover things about one of your parents that no one knew and that would bring embarrassment if their secret got out. What do you do?

If you discover something unsavory or unflattering about your parents, ask yourself the following questions:

- Does what I found offer absolute proof or only raise suspicions?
- Would what I found be considered evidence for any unsolved crime?

- If the information became public, would it implicate someone outside the family?

- Does anyone else have a right to know something my mother or father wanted to be kept secret?

- Will I be affected emotionally or spiritually trying to keep something secret from my siblings?

- If my mother or father went to great lengths to keep this secret, should I tell? (Think long and hard before you respond.)

I can't answer these questions for you, but as a general rule I would never recommend keeping something secret that might be illegal. In a case where I found hundreds of pounds of pharmaceuticals, I felt an obligation to contact the local narcotics department, but I did not pass the information on to surviving family members. When I have found sensitive materials such as pornographic magazines, I just toss them and say nothing because it is none of my business. It is particularly important to not judge others. Everyone reading this will have a different opinion as to how to handle these matters, which is why I am not recommending a specific course of action for any kind of discovery. But I hope my experiences and the questions I've raised for you will help you make your own decision should you discover an embarrassing family secret.

Principles of Personal Ethics

Ethical dilemmas rarely present themselves as such. They usually pass us by before we know it or develop so gradually we can only recognize them in hindsight—a little like noticing the snake after you've been bitten. But what are the signs that a snake might be present? An ethical framework is like a snake detector.

I offer the following principles as landmarks—generic indicators to be used as compelling guides for an active conscience. They are *not* absolute rules or values. They are more like a rough measurement where an exact one is not possible. They often conflict with each other in practice, and some will trump others under certain circumstances. But as principles that need to be considered, they appear constant.

In a sense, the principles are outcomes of the mother of all principles—unconditional love and compassion—which appear in virtually all faiths and are expressed here as concern for the well-being of others:

Respect for the autonomy of others
Trustworthiness and honesty
Willing compliance with the law
Basic justice; being fair
Refusing to take unfair advantage
Benevolence; doing good
Preventing harm[1]

When No One's Looking

Perhaps the most common challenge to our personal code of ethics comes with finding something valuable that no one knows about. For that matter, anything of sentimental or monetary value can present an opportunity to test our ethics. If you're in your parents' home alone and you see something you've always wanted, you may be tempted to slip it in your pocket and not say anything about it, especially if no one else is there. Chances are, you won't get caught, and you may have remembered your dad saying he wanted you to have it after he died.

Let's talk about you first. The grief and stress of losing a parent and then having to clear out the family home can play games with your otherwise meticulous ethical sensibilities. Greed, covetousness, and dishonesty can easily be translated to entitlement, especially if you're the one doing all the work. As you read this, I know you cannot imagine yourself taking something that doesn't belong to you, but I've seen good, honest people do worse things. If you slip a gold watch into your pocket, will you get away with it?

Probably. But then what? How will you deal with that knowledge? You're either going to have to keep the watch hidden forever from your siblings or sell it for cash. How is either of those choices going to make you feel?

If you're the executor of your parents' estate, you have a legal responsibility to settle your parents' affairs properly. But setting aside the legal requirements, when all is said and done, you have to live with yourself and sleep well at night. I strongly suggest that you *always* take the high road. If there's something you want that isn't covered in the will, go to your siblings and ask sincerely, using financial equity as your guiding principle.

What should you do if you see one of your siblings—or anyone else for that matter—sneak something off a table? The best insurance against that is to be diligent about protecting the property. I know it may have sounded extreme when I recommended it before, but it's always a good idea to either change the locks in your parents' home or make sure an entire home inventory has been documented so you can keep track of things. Never allow anyone in the house without you (or the executor) being present. Before your siblings go through the house, let them know you have an inventory and if there's anything on the list they want, they can let you know ahead of time. Knowing someone is monitoring the contents usually discourages anyone from a sudden case of sticky fingers.

But suppose you see your sister grab something and put it in her purse. You know your family better than I do, but usually a friendly, even humorous comment will do the trick: "I know you put that ring in your purse just to keep it warm, right?" What is she going to say? "Well, no, I'm actually trying to steal it!" By creating an atmosphere of trust from the beginning and wearing an attitude of friend rather than traffic cop, you will usually experience cooperation and trustworthiness.

Quiz—How Will You Handle Ethical Questions?

Take the following quiz to begin thinking about how you will handle ethical questions that come up as you clear out your parents' estate.

1. Your mother has Alzheimer's, and your father suffers from a heart condition and diabetes and has difficulty walking. They live in a two-story home that has become too difficult for them. However, they refuse to consider moving to a safer environment. What would you do?

   a. Try to reason with them and convince them to move.

   b. Have them declared physically incompetent, forcing them to move against their will.

   c. Trick them into moving to an assisted-living facility that you have secretly arranged for them.

2. Your mother recently passed away, and your father is still living with reasonably good health. He is not interested in selling or giving away anything that belonged to your mom. You have always wanted her sewing machine. What would you do?

   a. Ask your father if you could keep it at your house.

   b. Offer to buy it from your father.

   c. Make sure your siblings didn't want it, and then remove it from the home against your father's wishes.

3. Your father passed away three years ago, and your mother has recently died. You are the executor of the family estate. On your walk-through of the home, you notice several items of sentimental value that you would like to keep. What would you do?

   a. Make a list, and go over it with your siblings, asking permission to keep them.

   b. Take a few of the items but offer the rest to your siblings.

   c. Take what you want and say nothing to your siblings.

4. Your father is your last surviving parent. He is confused most of the time due to dementia. You have a close relationship with him and are named in his will as the executor. One day when you visit, he hands you an envelope with a dozen gold coins and tells you he wants you to have it. What do you do?

   a. Thank him and take them.

b.   Accept his gift but immediately contact your siblings and offer to divide them equally.

c.   Accept them, but add them to the will, indicating that they are to be divided equally with your siblings.

5.   Both of your parents have died, and you and your siblings are at the house, preparing to clear it out. When you walk past your parents' bedroom, you see your sister take a piece of costume jewelry of little value from your mother's dresser. What do you do?

a.   Ignore it because it has no resale value.

b.   Gently confront your sister and tell her you knew your mom would have wanted her to have it.

c.   Firmly but kindly tell her she can't take it unless all your siblings agree.

6.   Your father passed away, and your mom asked you to go through his clothes and other personal belongings. You notice a small box in the back of his sock drawer, and when you open it up, you see three romantic cards from another woman. What do you do?

a.   Remove the box of letters and destroy them, never mentioning it to anyone.

b.   Show it to your brother and ask him to promise never to mention it to anyone.

c.   Give the box to your mother.

7.   Your entire family is in the house, cleaning out all of the rooms. You find Mother's long-lost diamond ring in one of her purses. You have always wanted that ring, but so has you sister. What do you do?

a.   Announce to everyone you have found the ring in her purse.

b.   Tell your sister it has been found but since you found it, you are going to keep it.

c.   Put it in your pocket, thinking no one will ever know.

8. No one has been able to find Dad's will. You find it by accident inside an old magazine. The will stipulates that all of his estate is to go to his favorite charity, and none of it goes to his children. What do you do?

   a. Get rid of the evidence without including your siblings in that decision.

   b. Share it with your siblings and decide what to do.

   c. See to it that Dad's wishes are carried out.

No One *Tries* to Be a Problem

Naturally, you and your family need to abide by the highest ethical standards if you want to peacefully wrap up your parents' estate. But you can all be models of integrity and still run into problems. I have found that most people, particularly those struggling with the difficult emotions that surround the loss of a parent, really do want peace of mind and healing of the pain and anguish of the situation. They also want to get along with their loved ones. I really believe that, and while acting ethically will help, what you really need to practice is civility.

If you successfully graduated from kindergarten, you have already learned how to get through this—you *share*. As children, we all learned the golden rule: do unto others as you would have them do unto you.[2] Help each other. Be kind. Mind your manners. You might consider these the *softer* issues, but I have seen firsthand how they can turn a potential hurricane of discord into a sunny afternoon of delight. You see, you and your siblings are in a foreign land where you have to make quick decisions and face unknown challenges. But healing and peace of mind are right in front of you—in one another.

I know my major responsibility is to advise the family as to the best possible direction to take with their parents' personal property, but I try to help them through the emotional minefields as well, and my consistent advice is this: ooze kindness. Talk openly and calmly. Be generous with hugs. If you're standing next to your brother in the living room, reach over and grab his hand. Write down your feelings in a letter, and send it to your siblings. Call your sister out of the blue and just say, "I was thinking of you and hoping we could talk for a while. I miss you." When they all show up to go through the house, greet your brothers and sisters with a mug of their favorite coffee or tea.

I have seen the best and the worst of human behavior in helping people downsize and settle estates, and I've come to believe that success is a choice. You can be difficult, spiteful, and selfish, or you can choose the high road—not necessarily the easier road, but the better one for everyone and for your own peace of mind, knowing you did the right thing. As someone once said, kindness knows no enemies, and compassion knows no limits.

Kindness is also contagious. Model kindness from the get-go and watch your siblings try to outdo you (here's where sibling rivalry works positively). Remember that if you are hurting, your family is too. If someone insists on being cantankerous and tries to disrupt things, take the higher road anyway, and understand that his or her pain is not because of you. It's coming from a place of fear and not knowing how to process everything that is happening.

What Do I Do Now?

Current situation: any decision regarding your parents' health, safety, or possessions.

☑ *Do the right thing because it is the right thing to do.* If you are tempted to take something or you see a sibling pocket something, simply bring it out in the open in a nonconfrontational manner and talk it out. Honesty is always the best policy.

☑ *Get help from a trusted friend, spiritual counselor, or professional if you are struggling with an ethical issue.* If you discover something you find disturbing in your parents' home, I encourage you to talk to someone you really trust or seek counsel from a professional to help you understand your feelings.

☑ *Let bygones be bygones.* If you discover a secret that angers you about one of your parents, remember, you cannot fight with someone who is no longer alive. Sometimes someone else's secrets are better left buried to avoid further pain to family members.

Thirteen

I Will *Never* Do This to *My* Kids!

Even though I like to think of myself as a nice person, sometimes I have to get a little tough with my clients. Usually it happens when I have to referee disputes. In this chapter, I'm going to be tough with you, too, but it's for a good cause. I know you love your kids, and because I care about them, too, I'm going to nag you a little. For their sakes, and for yours, I'm going to risk being a little pushy and tell you, "Don't set your kids up for a big fight and a Dumpster load of ill feelings!"

I hope that everything in this book will help you write a beautiful final chapter to your parents' story—I hope the liquidation of their estate will have far fewer problems than those I see every day. But more than anything, I also hope you're willing to practice what you preach and will begin right now taking steps to give your kids the best final gift any parent can give: a peaceful final farewell and a loving legacy.

Remember I told you in chapter 3 how difficult it is for your parents to think about their own deaths? Well, it's a lot harder when you're in the prime of life. If you don't think so, try to imagine yourself experiencing dementia, or lying helpless on a bed in a nursing home, or hearing a doctor give you a year to live. Not very pleasant, I know. So even though we know intellectually that we won't live forever, emotionally we avoid thinking about the inevitable. But just for a few minutes, I'd like to gently remind you that your days are finite and that there are some things you can do right now to make sure you live those days focused on what really matters. That way, when your time comes, your family will have no reason to worry or fight over what you leave behind.

But I'm Only in My Fifties!

If you died tomorrow, is there a will to guide your family through the distribution of your property? According to most estimates, more than half of all Americans have not filled out a will, and my guess is that if you haven't filled out a will, you're uncomfortable doing it, so you keep putting it off. Who wants to go to an attorney to make out a will in their forties or fifties? Well, don't let that stop you because your attorney already knows the statistics and won't put you on a guilt trip when you make the appointment. And don't let cost become an excuse. Where there's a will, there's a way (pun intended).

While you're working on the will, designate someone in your family to be power of attorney. If you are a married person, the spouse is usually chosen, but not always. Can't decide who it will be and you don't want to hurt anyone's feelings? I know of a man who designated his two sons to have co-power of attorney. When their dad passed away, one of the brothers almost begged the other to take over, and everything went just fine. But before you select this option, though, let me caution you that co-powers of attorney are very tricky, especially if there is a difference of opinion. If you prefer to designate only one person, it's perfectly fine to select the one person who will get it done correctly, in a timely matter, and all the while holding the estate's best interests.

Next, do you have orderly files that contain all the important financial and legal information your survivors will need? Things like bank account numbers, investment accounts, and life insurance policies? If you pass away before your spouse, will he or she know where to find these things? If you outlive your spouse and die at a ripe old age, will your kids be able to close out your checking account? Spend an evening pulling all of this information together, put it in a safe place, and tell the right people where it is.

Seven Reasons to Get Rid of Your Own Stuff

1. You will experience less anxiety and worry about all the stuff you seldom use.
2. You will spend less time looking for things.
3. You will be helping people in need.
4. You will have more time to do what you *really* want to do.
5. You will find things you forgot you owned.
6. You will revitalize your routine with a new adventure.
7. You will protect your kids from ever having to do what you just did with your parents' home.

Simplify Your Own Estate

The next thing you can do to not burden your kids with the stress of clearing out your home is to begin to get a handle on it now. Simplifying your home has even become a bit of a fad, thanks to television programs geared toward helping people downsize. But even if you spread the work out over months or a couple of years, you will accomplish two things. First, you'll begin to enjoy life more by simplifying it, and second, your kids won't walk into a lifetime of clutter and be angry with *you*.

Admit it—you already have more stuff than you need and probably more than you can use. One of the differences between boomers and their parents is that boomers are addicted to leisure, despite being a generation that works longer hours than their parents ever did. Many of our homes have big front porches with rocking chairs, but when was the last time you saw a boomer wave from the front porch when you took your evening walk through the neighborhood? While I'm on this rant, do you know what one of the larger rooms in new homes is these days? Bathrooms. The home you grew up in probably had one small bathroom that somehow served your family well (and took less time to clean and maintain), but you probably have three, and your nest is either empty or close to it. My point is that we are blessed with more than our parents had, but we *enjoy life less*. So here's a really hard question to ponder: after your kids are out starting their own families, do you really need a five-bedroom home with three bathrooms and a garage full of stuff? Maybe it's time to shock your kids and buy a loft condo downtown so you can spend more time dancing than cleaning.

Of course, if you go to a smaller house, you'll need to get rid of some things. But even if you stay where you are, I'd like you to consider downsizing—not just to spare your kids the job but to enjoy a richer lifestyle. Be honest with yourself: does all that stuff packed in closets, the basement, and the garage enrich your life or pull you down when you think about it? I know, you don't think about it to avoid the hassle! Do you ever find yourself longing for the earlier years of your marriage when you didn't have much but had a lot of fun and adventure? Isn't it funny how we work so hard to get a bigger house and buy more things that promise fun and leisure and yet our lives feel busier and more harried with each passing year?

So why is it so hard for us to reduce our collection of stuff and simplify our lives? Here are a few reasons I have come across in my years of experience.

- One spouse is the hoarder, and to keep the peace, the other spouse just tolerates it.
- Clever advertising screams an irresistible message: you need to buy this to be happy!
- We can afford it. Middle-class incomes are at an all-time high.
- Even if we *can't* afford it, it's easy to buy stuff with just the swipe of a card (which is why credit card debt has become a national epidemic).
- Peer pressure doesn't stop at high school. If everyone in your social circle upgrades to a five-bedroom home, your previously adequate three-bedroom ranch seems too small.
- Blurred lines between needs and wants.

I suspect you already know if you've got too much stuff lying around or need to downsize your home, but here are some indicators to help you make your decision:

- When I go to hang up a shirt or blouse in the closet, I have to push apart the other clothes to make space.
- I can't see the floor in my closets.
- All of our kids have moved out.
- At least one bedroom has been turned into a storage area.
- We rent storage space or have filled a small storage barn.
- We have at least two empty bedrooms that are seldom used.
- There are more licensed vehicles than licensed drivers at our home.
- We have more than one credit card, and on at least one we are only paying the minimum balance each month.
- We can't put our vehicles in the garage because we use it for storage.

The nice thing about simplifying your lifestyle is that you don't have to do it in a day or two. Remember, it took you ten to twenty years to fill that house, so if you gradually begin to get rid of things you don't need or use that often, you'll have a clutter-free home in just a few months.

Before you begin, set aside space or an empty box for items in each of these three categories: *keep, donate,* and *throw away.* Then start just as you did when you cleaned out your parents' home: climb into the attic and find a new home for everything you carted up there. Most of that stuff could be labeled "someday," as in "Someday I'll make a quilt out of all my kids' old flannel shirts." Well, either make someday today and get started on that quilt, or be honest with yourself and admit that quilt will never come to be. Load up your SUV with all the quilts, jeans, sweaters, and jackets and make a nice donation so a less-fortunate family can keep their own kids well dressed. And don't fool yourself into thinking your grandkids will wear those clothes someday. First, those kids already have everything they need and want. Second, do you really think your granddaughter wants to wear her mom's clothes when she goes into the eighth grade?

My first rule of downsizing for boomers: keep an empty attic.

If attics are for someday, our closets are for *just in case*. When you stop to think about it, you really need only about three or four pairs of shoes at any given time. But when you buy a new pair, you always keep the old pair just in case. Before you know it, you've got twenty pairs of shoes taking up space in your closet. For men, it's neckties. I don't know what it is about men, but many still have ties they wore in college and will never wear again, but they keep them on that overloaded tie rack in the closet. So after you've cleared out the attic, attack your closets and dressers, but don't store the extras in the attic. One of the perennial needs at homeless shelters is shoes—gather every pair you haven't worn or don't like and make sure the homeless in your city at least have one nice pair of shoes.

Continue the top-down process, moving from the attic to the upper floor, main floor, basement, and garage. Try to set a goal of one room a month, and stick with it. For most homes, that means you'll be completely clutter-free within a year!

The Zero-Sum Game

It's not too late to stem the tide of clutter in your own home. Here's a little game you and your spouse can play.

Aside from your basic grocery shopping, never purchase anything without getting rid of something else. If something new comes into your house, make a promise something else leaves. For example, if you buy a pair of shoes, drop off a pair at a homeless shelter (one of the biggest needs for these shelters is shoes). If you buy a new suit, get rid of an old one. In most cases, you already have more than enough of almost every category of possessions.

Bonus activity: for every bag of purchases you bring home from the mall, get rid of two bags of stuff. Over time, you will gradually downsize without even knowing it.

Is It Time to Move?

Getting rid of excess baggage is one thing; keeping your house from filling back up with clutter is another. One reason we accumulate is that some of us have the room for it—all those clean closets and empty spaces are soon begging to be refilled. So this is a good time to ask yourself if you really need all that space.

One of the most difficult decisions for baby boomers is whether or not to move into a smaller, more efficient home, yet there's a trend of boomers opting for townhomes and condos. The biggest hurdle to moving to a smaller home revolves around your children: "Will I have enough room for my children to visit with my grandchildren?" That is an important factor, but try to consider it from a practical perspective. How often do all of your kids return? Usually, the whole clan only gathers for a couple of holidays, and maintaining four thousand square feet is a big price to pay for one or two visits. Keep in mind you don't need to move into a tiny one-bedroom apartment. Going from a large two-story home with five bedrooms to a comfortable ranch with three will still give you plenty of room for your family gatherings. Also, the designs of the newer condos might surprise you with their ability to entertain large groups. If you have even the slightest inclination to consider moving to a smaller home but are worried about space issues, spend a weekend touring open houses for smaller houses and condos—usually the "Will I have enough room?" issue is a nonissue.

Moving into a smaller home isn't for everyone, but reducing clutter is. You have or will soon experience the daunting challenging of clearing out a family home filled with a lifetime of accumulation, and you don't want to do that to your own children. But that's a long way off. The benefits of getting rid of excess property begin immediately, allowing you to enjoy life more and worry less. So what's stopping you?

What Do I Do Now?

Current situation: within two months of completing the liquidation of your parents' estate.

☑ *Do the numbers.* Subtract your current age from the number seventy-five (men) or eighty (women). According to national averages, that's how much longer you may live.

☑ *Check your will.* Do you have one? If not, there's no time like the present. If you have one but haven't updated it in five years, consider updating it.

☑ *Climb into your attic.* Take a look in your attic and clear out anything unnecessary.

☑ *Reduce your personal belongings by at least 20 percent.* If you have twenty pairs of shoes, get rid of at least four. And so on.

☑ *House shop.* Spend at least one weekend viewing smaller houses, condos, or apartments.

Fourteen

Be Good to Yourself

We baby boomers struggle with one of the great paradoxes of life. On the one hand, these really are the best years of our lives. For most of us, we've arrived at a level of income that allows us to live comfortably, and despite occasional hiccups in the economy, we're living in an era of unprecedented opportunity. We're well past the diaper days and enjoy watching our children blossom and move out on their own. We seem to have less leisure time but more money to enjoy travel and pursue various hobbies and interests. Compared to where we were twenty years ago, life is pretty good.

On the other hand, we're hearing the first whispers of our own mortality as we watch our parents age. Our kids still need our support, but now our parents do too. And then when the last parent passes away, the emotional and physical stress seem overwhelming.

So I'd like to remind you of something I learned in my years of working with people going through this stressful time: helpers need help too. When you lose your parents, your life momentarily turns upside down. Yes, this, too, shall pass, but while you're in the middle of the storm, it seems as though you'll never see the sun shine again. I'm here to tell you it not only will shine again someday but also peek through as you handle all the details of closing out your parents' lives.

If you are the executor of your parents' estate, you have a particularly heavy burden, leaving yourself open to criticism, jealousy, and hard feelings as you devote months to handling all the details. But even if you do not have those responsibilities, this is not an easy time for you. Here are some ways to cope with all that you will feel and experience.

You're All You've Got

Sometimes after experiencing the loss of a parent or both parents, you realize how much your children and spouse mean to you. A few boomers have been known to say, "They're all I've got now," meaning they could no longer go to their parents for advice or help and, in fact, would now be the patriarch or matriarch for their children and grandchildren. This can be daunting, but it can also be comforting if you turn to your family for support.

Even in the rush of planning a funeral, greeting relatives, and eventually settling the estate, make sure you carve out some time with your spouse and children. Those who study the effects of stress on marriages report that the death of a parent can put a great strain on a good marriage, so pay particular attention to your spouse. Go on at least one date, and try not to focus on the events surrounding your parent's death. Your spouse may not fully understand what you are going through, but whatever help he or she tries to give will be done with the best intentions, so receive it graciously.

Keep in mind that men especially tend to shut down emotionally, keeping their feelings to themselves when what they really need is a close friend to walk with them through their grief and distress. You can be that friend, but be careful about trying to force your husband to open up. Just be there by his side, and hold his hand more than you normally do. He may not readily acknowledge it, but those small acts of tenderness will mean everything to him.

Special attention needs to be given to your children, and meeting their needs will comfort both you and them. If you open up and share your grief at losing a parent with theirs over losing a grandparent, you will connect in ways that will help both of you. I know of a woman who sat on her teenage daughter's bed the night after her father's funeral and asked her, "What will you remember most about Grandpa?" She said they talked for two hours, and while there were tears, there was also laughter. "She didn't realize it, but my daughter became my grief counselor that night," the mom reported. Even if your family has experienced more than the usual amount of discord, they can become your greatest resource during this time. You just need to let them.

I've mentioned several times that good, consistent communication and togetherness will smooth out the rough edges of handling your parents' affairs. Well, it shouldn't end after the house is emptied. Do your best to stay in touch with your siblings in the weeks and months after the funeral. Don't hesitate to pick up the phone and dial your brother or sister when you're feeling particularly sad. Chances are they will welcome a shoulder to cry on as they offer you theirs. I know of a family that celebrated their parents' wedding anniversary two months after the last funeral. Find ways to get together as an extended family, especially during the first year following your parents' deaths, not merely to remember your parents but to strengthen the bonds between you and your siblings. Like it or not, you really have become the patriarchs and matriarchs for your family, and you will gain strength from your new role, realizing that others are looking to you for direction.

Self-Care

It goes without saying that you need to pay attention to your physical and emotional health during the time from your parents' final days until the estate is successfully liquidated. This is especially true if a lengthy illness is involved. You may find yourself making numerous long trips to take your turn at the hospital or at their bedside while still trying to manage your own life and family responsibilities. This period presents what I refer to as *ticking time bombs* that can explode into everything from arguments to physical illness. Here are some of the more common time bombs to watch for:

- *Guilt.* Over missing soccer games, birthdays, vacations; over not being there when Mom took a turn for the worse.

- *Anger.* No matter how hard you try, you will get angry; usually at your spouse for not being understanding enough but also at your kids, your parent, a doctor, or health care professional.

- *Depression.* Not just sadness but something close to clinical depression—when you hardly have the energy to get out of bed, let alone make that long drive to visit your parent.

- *Fatigue.* Long nights without sleep, too tired to do anything.

- *Loneliness.* Many times, you will be all by yourself, and the prospect of losing your parent only intensifies the feeling that you're alone.

- *Illness.* Lack of sleep, stress, and poor diet can affect your resistance to colds, flu, and stomach and digestive problems.

- *Fear.* Thinking things like, *What am I going to do without Dad? What if I make the wrong decision as executor of his will? What's going to happen with the huge debt he left?*

I call these time bombs because we never know when they will hit. For example, you could have enjoyed a wonderful visit with your mom as she convalesces in the hospital, but on the drive home you may be hit with a huge sense of loneliness. Or out of the blue you might snap at your spouse. These things will happen, but there are some things you can do to help yourself.

Pay attention to the little things, such as sleep, nutrition, and exercise. If you're spending time visiting a seriously ill parent in the hospital, go outside and take a brisk ten-minute walk every hour or so. If you belong to a health club or exercise regularly, do your best to stick with your exercise routine. Exercise is one of the best defenses against these time bombs, but it's usually one of the first things we give up when in crisis situations.

Even if you don't feel like eating, try to get at least one good meal each day and supplement that with regular healthy snacks throughout the day. Avoid fried and fatty or rich foods; they only exacerbate any digestive problems that seem to go with stress. When my work has me on the run for several days—and believe me, I experience some of the same emotions as my clients—I keep a bag of trail mix or granola bars handy to keep my energy level up.

Sleep is one of the first things to go in stressful situations, even though you may feel tired all the time. Since your body is truly tired, you probably don't need sleep aids at this point. Instead, try to do something relaxing such as reading or listening to music before you go to bed. Avoid big meals or strenuous exercise close to bedtime, and don't stay in bed tossing and turning. Get up, write a letter to your brother or sister, and then climb back in bed. I love the idea of catnaps. So if you feel drowsy during the day, find a couch or comfortable chair and catch a few minutes of sleep. It's not a substitute for a full night's sleep, but it will minimize fatigue.

One of your best allies in coping with these time bombs is your primary care physician. Schedule an appointment, and let your doctor know what you're experiencing. He may prescribe a mild antidepressant or sleep aid, and he will also check your blood pressure and heart rate to either discover something that can be easily treated or leave you with peace of mind that physically you're fine. If you experience any of the following symptoms, mention them to your doctor:

- Headaches
- Stomach upset or digestive problems
- Muscle tension or pain
- Chest pain/irregular heartbeat
- Weight gain/loss
- Shortness of breath
- Skin problems
- Teeth grinding/jaw clenching

These *could* be symptoms of an actual medical problem that needs to be addressed, but most likely they are related to the stress you are experiencing, so practicing one or more of the following stress-reduction techniques will either eliminate or reduce their effects.

Deep breathing. Several times a day, sit in a comfortable chair or relax on a couch and breathe deeply for at least two minutes. To make sure you're breathing properly with your diaphragm, put one hand on your stomach and one on your chest. As you inhale, the hand on your stomach should rise a little while the hand on your chest should not.

Progressive muscle relaxation. Beginning with your toes and moving up your body, clench your toes for five seconds, and then let them relax as completely as possible for five seconds. Then do this with your leg muscles, your stomach muscles, your hands, arms, and so on.

Meditation and prayer. Meditation is simply sitting very still, blocking out all distracting thoughts, and focusing on something inspirational. Prayer is talking to God and listening. The point of both is to focus on higher thoughts, allowing them to block any negative or stressful things you're dealing with.

Massage. Treat yourself to an hour massage at a day spa or health club. But if those aren't available, ask your spouse to give you a massage and don't hesitate to guide the process to places where tension sits, as in the neck and shoulders. You can even give yourself a partial massage—a vigorous scalp massage being the easiest.

Exercise. As I previously mentioned, exercise is a great way to relieve stress, and it will also minimize the symptoms related to stress. Don't think of exercise as running five miles or swimming for an hour. Walking is probably the best and easiest exercise for relieving stress-related symptoms. You can also put on some music and dance in your living room. Believe it or not, even housework qualifies as exercise. If you're a golfer, tennis player, or play a team sport in a community league, keep your regular schedule.

Spiritual Self-Care

- Make time for reflection.
- Spend time with nature.
- Find a spiritual connection or community.
- Be open to inspiration.
- Cherish your optimism and hope.
- Surround yourself with kind, loving people.

- Be aware of nonmaterial aspects of life.

- Try at times not to be in charge or the expert.

- Be open to not knowing.

- Identify what is meaningful to you and notice its place in your life.

- Meditate.

- Pray.

- Sing.

- Spend time with children.

- Have experiences of awe.

- Contribute to causes in which you believe.

- Read Scripture and inspirational literature.

You're a Social Being

There's one final deterrent to the harmful effects of the grief and stress you will experience, and it may be the most important: other people—your family, obviously, but others as well. If you're a boomer, you probably remember the lyrics to the Beatles' song "With a Little Help from My Friends."[1] The poet Emily Dickinson put it this way: "My friends are my estate."[2] And from the ancient wisdom of the Old Testament, we read, "Two are better than one, because they have a good reward for their labor. For if they fall, one will lift up his companion. But woe to him who is alone when he falls; for he has no one to help him up."[3]

I recall a gentleman once telling me he didn't want to be a burden on his friends. But when you stop and think about it, the best gift you can give a friend is your trust. I guarantee that if you have a close friend who knows what you're going through, he or she will want to help you. Call your best friend whenever the burden seems too much to carry. Make a list right now of at least three close friends, or better yet, make sure their phone numbers are programmed into your cell phone.

In addition to your very close friends, it will help you to be around other people. If you are part of a church or other religious community, share your situation with them. I can really only speak for myself, but here in the South, you can't have a death in the family without being flooded with casseroles, cards, hugs, and offers of help. Those expressions of kindness and compassion will bring tremendous comfort to you and your family. Many churches even have teams of people trained to help others through times of grief or trauma. Most religious organizations have a prayer chain, which is a group of people who go into action whenever someone calls with a need. It's extremely comforting to know other people are praying for you throughout your difficult journey. Other religious communities offer counseling, and leaders of those communities often try to make personal visits to encourage and counsel. But none of this will happen if you keep to yourself. Reach out to others and feel their kindness when you need it most.

You also may benefit from seeking the professional help of a counselor or therapist. Several studies have pointed out that following traumatic events such as the 9/11 terrorist attack, people most directly affected by the trauma do not believe they need professional help and do not seek it when it's recommended. They give at least three reasons: others are worse off than they are, seeking help is a sign of weakness, and they rely solely on family and friends. I'm not comparing the death of your parents to a terrorist attack, but your emotions could easily move from sadness to clinical depression and anxiety. If the strategies I've outlined don't seem to be working, consider seeking professional help from a licensed therapist. Counseling of this nature is generally covered by your health insurance.

Celebration as an Antidote to Sorrow

Finally, even though these may be the deepest days of sorrow you have ever faced, some of that sorrow can be lightened by fond memories of your loved one. For many, a funeral can be a celebration of life, an opportunity to share inspiring stories about your loved one's accomplishments, how he lived, and how he touched people during his life. Focusing your thoughts on positive memories, as well as reminiscing with friends and family about the fun times you shared with your loved one, will help you through these difficult days.

Even if you experience a long and drawn-out death vigil as your parent slowly slips away, you owe it to yourself and your family to balance your sadness with some fun. Go to a movie (comedies, please), take your family out for ice cream, go bowling, or just make a big bowl of popcorn and play cards some evening. I hope this advice doesn't sound disrespectful because that is not my intent. But I'll bet your parents would have you doing something fun rather than sitting around grieving all the time. More important, you will be stronger and more capable of taking care of the responsibilities facing you. The American poet Karl Shapiro wrote, "Laughter and grief join hands."[4] I think he understood that even in the darkest of times, people need to laugh. And as the late Norman Cousins learned from his own experience of renting funny movies while being treated for an incurable disease, laughter has tremendous healing power. After several weeks of watching old Marx brothers films, his disease went into an inexplicable remission; he then went on to devote the rest of his life to the relationship of personal attitude to health.[5]

The journey from your parents' first signs of decline to the day their house is finally emptied may be long and difficult, filled with more stress and sorrow than you deserve. You may feel that helping yourself is impossible because of the urgency of the situation, the sadness of the moment, and your own sense of responsibility to put others first. So I'd like to close this chapter with a simple request: pledge to yourself right now that you will do at least one helpful thing for yourself each day.

What Do I Do Now?

Current situation: anytime from the first signs of your parents' physical decline.

☑ Call your best friend and tell him/her what's going on with your parents.

☑ Engage your favorite hobby or pastime at least once this week (golf, fishing, gardening, scrapbooking).

☑ Meditate or pray for five minutes.

☑ Go out for an evening of dining and dancing with your spouse or a friend this week.

Fifteen

Mission Accomplished!

In many ways, this has not been an easy book to write, and I'm sure parts of it were as difficult to read. No one enjoys thinking about and making plans for their parents' deaths, but because I see what happens when people don't prepare for the inevitable, I wanted to share everything I've learned through my experiences and the lives of my clients. I truly believe if you put into practice what you have learned, you will successfully walk with your family through this difficult journey and look back on it as a wonderful privilege. If you read this while your parents are still reasonably healthy, you will have had that conversation with them, avoiding much of the conflict and heartache that comes when you're not prepared. If you bought this book close to your parents' passing, you will have been able to get through the remaining challenges with minimal discord and difficulty. Now I would like to leave you with one final strategy that will literally close the book on this chapter of your life and leave you with great memories to cherish: how to truly celebrate your parents' lives.

Remember that funerals are celebrations. They are opportunities for the rest of us to honor our memories of the deceased. Encourage those who will make tributes to try to include a humorous story to give others a chance to laugh. I heard of one tribute that went something like this: "You may wonder why we are having this funeral so early in the morning, but Dad was such a State fan, he wanted to make sure you all had time to get back home and cheer them on today." Another said, "I think it's more than ironic that Mom died the day after the new Medicare rules went into effect. She hated all that paperwork and probably just said, 'To heck with it!' and left for a better place."

Dr. Kenneth Taylor, the man who translated the King James Bible into the best-selling *Living Bible,* took an active role in planning his own funeral. Among other things, his grandchildren and their spouses—all musically gifted—sang as a beautiful choir during the service. And believe it or not, he had made a videotape of himself just for his funeral, treating the entire congregation to a comforting and inspiring message.[1] I share these examples only to underscore the importance of planning ahead to give your mom and dad the celebrations they deserve. If your parents did not share any funeral plans with you, join with your siblings and plan an event that communicates your love for them and their uniqueness to others.

Keeping Their Memory Alive

A few weeks ago, one of the television networks ran a special news segment about three boys who lost their father when they were too young to have much of a memory of him. Apparently the father drowned at sea, and the ship he was on was never found. Yet some forty years later, his three sons led an expedition that found the ship and brought closure to the family. I remember thinking when I heard about this story, *How wonderful that these boys who scarcely knew their father kept his memory alive for so long.*

Over the years, I have heard of many special ways that families keep the memories of their parents alive and would like to end this book by sharing them with you. I know how hard it may be for you to do many of the things I have suggested, so do yourself and your family a favor by coming up with a way to continue to enjoy your parents forever. Honor them always.

Plant a tree. Shortly after the interment service, one family gathered in front of the assisted-living center where both parents spent their final years together. One of the sons brought a shovel, and everyone—siblings, nephews and nieces, grandkids, and even great-grandkids, took a turn at digging a hole. Then, a lovely silver maple—their mom's favorite tree—was lifted into the hole, and again, everyone took a turn shoveling the dirt back into the hole. By the time they were done, a crowd of nurses and residents had gathered and began clapping. That tree will not only remind everyone at the facility how much they enjoyed knowing that elderly couple, but every time family members visit the gravesite, they can drive a few blocks to the assisted-living center and see the tree they planted in memory of their loved one.

Distribute cuttings. Sally loved her African violets and took great pride in caring for them in their colorful pots on the ledge of the big bay window in her living room. After she passed away, one of her daughters pulled off several dozen cuttings from the plants and started them in a bowl of water. Once they developed roots, she planted each cutting in a little clay pot with *Mom* or *Grandma* hand-painted on the side and gave them to all her siblings and their children. As far as I know, to this day—several years after Sally died—her memory lives on in homes, dorm rooms, and apartments all over the country.

Share favorite recipes. Another creative daughter went through her mother's recipe box and picked out about a dozen signature recipes her mom was known for. She used her computer to create a small recipe book and gave it to everyone in the family.

Keep the fishing trip alive. Harold took his two sons on a fly-in fishing trip in remote Ontario every spring. The spring after his death, those sons planned a fishing trip with their own sons and daughters and spent at least one evening around the campfire, telling fish stories about their dad. It has now become an annual tradition.

Create a memory book. Remember all those boxes of photos you found when you cleared out your parents' home? One enterprising son selected several dozen pictures of his parents, from their wedding picture through various stages and memorable events of their lives, scanned them onto his computer, and put together a lovely memory book that gets circulated among his siblings. In another family, old home movies were transferred to DVDs and copies were given to family members. This makes so much more sense than just carting those boxes into your own attic where no one will ever get to enjoy the photos.

Give a lifelong gift. Many families contribute to charities and causes in memory of their parents. Often those charities provide a visible way to display these gifts. And you don't have to be extremely wealthy and have a building named after your parents. One family pays for a scholarship for one under-privileged child to be able to go to a YMCA day camp in their city—with the name of the parent attached to the scholarship.

Make a family DVD. Local video companies can document and film your parents talking about their own lives prior to their passing and have copies made for everyone. Take it out once a year and review it to remember their own words and feelings.

Re-create your parents' presence. There are a lot of ways to do this. One daughter remembered that every time she was around her dad, she loved the smell of his Old Spice aftershave lotion. So she kept a bottle around, and every now and then, the Old Spice would remind her of him. Another son recalled how his mom loved listening to Glenn Miller. It took some doing with a lot of help from iTunes, but eventually he collected enough songs to burn CDs for his family members so they could remember what it was like to walk into Mom's house.

You're Never Alone

Even after their passing, your parents will always be Mom and Dad to you. Physically, they have left this earth, but I believe their memory will live on forever. Just as you were blessed to have them with you through all those years, you will be blessed to keep them alive in your heart.

Every step of the journey—from the darkness of their first signs of decline to the clearing out of their house, to the details of planning their funerals—provides you with a choice. You can focus on the sadness and inconvenience of settling their affairs, or you can let each event remind you of their contri-bution in your life. They molded *you*, remember? You might think my job is depressing, but I love it because I'm usually able to see the ending of the dark period and the light of hope that comes back to you through this process. It is my hope that I've turned on many lights for you and that you enjoy for-ever the memory of one of the greatest gifts we are given: our parents.

What Do I Do Now?

Current situation: your parents have both passed away.

☑ Make sure you have a plan for your parents' funerals.

☑ Choose at least one way to keep your parents' memories alive.

☑ Give this book to someone who needs it.

Appendix A

Your Complete Parent Care Checklist

1. When your parent(s) are in good health and living independently . . .

   - Ask if they have an updated will and if they've named an executor.

   - Encourage them to meet with a financial planner and estate planning attourney.

   - Ask them if they have made any decisions for when they might not be able to care for themselves.

   - Encourage them to begin sorting through the things they have collected over the years.

   - Remind them—often—that you love them.

2. When your parents begin to show signs of deteriorating health . . .

   - Along with your siblings, try to visit regularly.

   - Begin keeping a record of any noticeable changes or health emergencies (falls, trips to the emergency room, memory lapses).

   - Research potential assistance in their area (Meals on Wheels, home health care nurse).

- Obtain phone numbers of at least one neighbor, and let the neighbors know your parents are experiencing health problems.
- If you live close to them, offer to assist with bill paying, grocery shopping, trips to the doctor, and other household duties.
- Meet with your siblings to begin a conversation about your parents' future.
- Make sure you and your siblings have a communication plan if either of your parents experiences a health emergency.
- Remind them—often—that you love them.

3. When one parent dies . . .
   - Offer to assist your surviving parent with funeral preparations.
   - Have a conversation with your parent about his or her living arrangements, and then support that parents' wishes.
   - With your siblings, visit regularly to make sure your parent is safe and healthy and to help fill the void from the loss of a lifetime companion.
   - Offer to assist your parent in sorting through things that have been collected over the years.
   - Consider options for assistance should your parent need it.
   - Remind your parent—often—of your love.

4. When your last surviving parent dies . . .
   - Send appropriate notices to extended family, friends, and clergy from your parent's church or synagogue. If donations to a charity are preferred to flowers, indicate that in the announcement.
   - With your siblings, plan the funeral according to your parent's wishes.
   - Consult with the funeral director regarding any arrangements made for payment.

- Make sure the home is securely locked (if there is a pet, make arrangements to care for the pet). Contact local law enforcement and inform them that the house will be vacant.

- Meet briefly with your siblings to arrange a date to make decisions regarding the liquidation of your parents' estate and to review the will with the executor.

5. When you meet with your siblings after the funeral of your last surviving parent . . .

- Allow time for mutual support, expressing sadness, recalling fond memories.

- Review the will with the executor and agree to execute it exactly as written. If an attourney is involved, contact him immediately.

- Locate all financial records, contracts, titles, and other important paperwork.

- Contact the financial planner, any banks, financial institutions, and investment and insurance companies with whom your parents did business and close out all accounts as determined by the will.

- Determine how debts are to be paid off.

- Following the guidelines in chapter 8, determine if you will have an estate sale, auction, or donate the contents of the home.

- Consider hiring a personal property appraiser to identify the monetary value of significant items in the home.

- Determine if you will clear out the home yourselves or hire a professional (see chapter 11).

- If you decide to have an estate sale or auction, contact a professional who performs these services and set a date for the event.

- If you decide to donate the contents of the home, contact the charity of your choice.

- Set a date for clearing the home of all its contents.

- If the home is to be sold, contact a Realtor.
- Do your part in modeling a generous and cooperative spirit to each of your siblings.

6. Clearing out your parents' home . . .

Prior to the appointed day to clear out the home:

- Contact a refuse hauling service and inform them when additional trash will be placed at the curb. Consult with the service about proper procedures for handling toxic substances, such as old paint, solvents, and chemicals.
- Contact a local shredding company if there is a large supply of important papers.
- Make arrangements for lawn care until the home is occupied.
- Determine how many people will be assisting, and make sure you have enough food and drinks for everyone.
- Also make sure you have an adequate supply of the following:
  * large, heavy-duty trash bags
  * work gloves and rubber gloves
  * masks to protect from dust
  * safety glasses or some other form of eye protection
  * tools for disassembling furniture
  * cleaning supplies
  * wasp or insect spray
  * hand truck for moving large items
  * piano mover if your parents owned a piano
  * flashlights and at least one trouble light (the type used by auto mechanics)
  * stepladder and at least one smaller step stool
  * first-aid kit to treat minor scrapes

* bottled drinking water

* spackling compound to fill holes from removing pictures from the walls

* cardboard boxes for books

* automatic timer to set a lamp to come on at night

- Notify your parents' neighbors of your plans.

- Arrange for a pickup truck or utility trailer for moving larger items that family members want to keep.

The day of the clearing of your parents' home:

- Allow everyone some time to walk through the home and identify anything else they would like to keep—if there are disputes, see chapter 8 for ways to resolve them. Make sure everyone knows these items need to be removed from the property that day.

- Create a comfortable atmosphere with music, snacks, and favorite photos of your parents.

- Determine which rooms will be used to collect things to save, things to donate, and things to discard.

- Assign teams of at least two to various rooms, beginning with the attic and moving down.

- Instruct everyone to look carefully for any hidden treasure (see chapter 11).

- As each room is cleared, make sure it is also cleaned thoroughly (floors vacuumed or washed, sinks and lavatories cleaned, and so on)—a professional cleaning company could be hired to provide this service.

- Once the home is completely cleared out, walk through one more time to make sure nothing is left behind.

- Connect a lamp in the living room to a timer to come on at night.

- Turn off all other lights and electrical devices, and set the thermostat at an appropriate temperature to conserve energy.
- Lock all doors, and make sure windows are also secure.

Appendix B

Helpful Resources

The Internet is a great place to look for help with specific issues relating to caring for your aging parents and liquidating their estate. Here's a list of places to start.

To find elder-law attorneys, appraisers, financial planners, and other professionals to assist you or your parents:

www.search-attorneys.com

www.fpanet.org (financial planners)

www.aselonline.com (American Society of Estate Liquidators)

www.auctioneers.org (National Association of Auctioneers)

www.appraisers.org (American Society of Appraisers)

www.isa-appraisers.org/ISA_form.html (International Society of Appraisers)

www.shredit.com (shredding service)

www.recycle.net/trade/aa995019.html (help in getting rid of junk)

www.optoutprescreen.com (stop unwanted mail)

www.napo.net (National Association of Professional Organizers)

www.naela.org (National Academy of Elder Law Attorneys)

Organizations that can provide information and direct you to further resources in helping you care for your elderly parents:

AARP (www.aarp.org)—National Web site for the American Association of Retired Persons that provides education, advocacy, and research

AARP Driver Safety Program (www.aarp.org/drive)—To locate a refresher driving program in your area

Administration on Aging (www.aoa.gov or 202-619-0724)—Elder-care ideas, topics, elder abuse, LTC ombudsman

Agenet (www.agenet.com)—Information for the elderly, including financial, legal, health care, and other advice

Aging Solutions (www.Aging-Parents-and-Elder-Care.com)—Articles, comprehensive checklists, and links to key resources designed to make it easier for people caring for an aging parent or elderly spouse to quickly find the information they need

Alzheimer's Association (www.alz.org or 704-532-7392)

Alzinfo.org (www.alzinfo.org)—Comprehensive information about Alzheimer's disease

American Association of Homes and Services for the Aging (AAHSA) (www.aahsa.org or 202-783-2242)

American Bar Association Commission on Law and Aging (www.abanet.org or 202-662-1000)—Health and financial decisions, legal tools for preserving your autonomy

American Cancer Society (www.cancer.org or 800-232-2345)

American Heart Association (www.americanheart.com)—Information on heart disease as well as local chapter information

Assisted Living Federation of America (www.alfa.org or 703-691-8100)—Consumer information on elder housing options, services, and protections

Benefits Checkup (www.BenefitsCheckUp.org)—A free, easy-to-use service that identifies federal and state assistance programs for older Americans

Better Business Bureau Foundation (www.bbbconsumerfoundation.org)— Provides information about consumer frauds and scams and tips for prevention

Careguide.com (www.careguide.com)—Resources about aging and elder care, ranging from support with daily living to financial and legal information as well as community support

Center for Family Caregivers (www.familycaregivers.org)

Center for LTC Financing (www.centerltc.org)

Center for Medicare Education (www.medicareed.org)—Includes info on Medicare Part D

Children of Aging Parents (www.caps4caregivers.org or 800-227-7294)—Information, resources, and referrals for caregivers of aging parents

Eldercare Locator (800-677-1116)—The Eldercare Locator can put you in contact with the Office for the Aging in your area, which provides help in locating needed services in your area (a service administered by the National Association of Area Agencies on Aging and the National Association of State Units on Aging)

Eldercare Online (www.ec-online.net)—Whether you are caring for a spouse, parent, relative, or neighbor, this is an online community where supportive peers and professionals help you improve quality of life for yourself and your elder

Elderlyabuse.com (www.elderlyabuse.com)—Committed to help fight any abuse—physical, emotional, or financial—working to educate the public about the misuse of guardianships imposed on elders, which wrongly strips them of all rights and assets

Elderweb (www.elderweb.com)—Locating records and property

Ethicalwill.com (www.ethicalwill.com)—Information on creating an ethical will

Extended Care Info Network (www.elderconnect.com)—Detailed directory of long-term care providers, home health agencies, retirement communities, hospices, and nursing homes; searchable by city, county, state, type of facility, or institution name; also lists related Internet resources

Family Care Resource Connection (www.caregiving.org)

Family Caregiver Alliance (www.caregiver.org or 415-434-3388)—Offering information, education, and support to families caring for loved ones

Firstgov (www.seniors.gov)—Access to government Web sites

Foundation Aiding the Elderly (www.4fate.org)—Assuring our elders are treated with care, dignity, and the utmost respect during their final years when they can no longer take care of themselves

Health Compass (www.healthcompass.org)

Hospice Foundation of America (www.hospicefoundation.org or 800-854-3402)—Information on Medicare, managed care, Medigap insurance, long-term care insurance, long-term care facilities, and reports on health care fraud prevention programs

Kaiser Family Foundation (www.kif.org or 202-347-5270)—Talking with your parents about Medicare and health coverage

Medicaid (www.cms.hhs.gov/consumers)

Medicare (www.medicare.gov or 800-633-4227)

Medicare Nursing Home Ratings (www.medicare.gov/Nhcompare/Home.asp)—A tool that enables you to read about ratings of local nursing homes in your area

Medicare Rx Education (www.medicarerxeducation.org)—Thorough information about the prescription drug plan changes

National Adult Day Services Association (NADSA) (www.nadsa.org or 866-890-7357)

National Alliance for Caregiving (www.caregiving.org)

National Association for Home Care (www.nahc.org or 202-547-7424)—Advises on selecting a home care or hospice provider and locates agencies in the area

National Association of Geriatric Care Managers (www.caremanager.org)

National Center for Assisted Living (www.ncal.org or 202-842-4444)—Information on all aspects of assisted living and residential care facilities

National Citizens' Coalition for Nursing Home Reform (www.nccnhr.org or 202-332-2275)

National Council on Patient Information and Education (www.talkaboutrx.org or 301-656-8565)—Questions to ask when taking prescription and nonprescription medicines and how to talk about using them safely

National Council on the Aging (www.ncoa.org or 202-479-1200)—Organizations and professionals dedicated to promoting the dignity, self-determination, and well-being of older persons

National Family Caregivers Association (NFCA) (www.nfcacares.org or 800-896-3650)

National Institutes of Health (www.nih.gov/health)

National Mental Health Association (www.nmha.org or 800-969-6642)—Free information about mental health, mental illness, and local treatment facilities

National Parkinson Foundation, Inc. (www.parkinson.org or 800-327-4545)

National Transit Resource Center (800-527-8279)—Provides referrals for transportation for seniors

Ourelders.org (www.ourelders.org)—Comprehensive links to Web sites with information and resources for the elderly as well as information on links to Alzheimer's disease-related sites

Social Security Administration Online (www.ssa.gov)

U.S. Department of Health and Human Services (www.hhs.gov or 877-696-6775)—U.S. agency for protecting the health of U.S. residents

United States Administration on Aging, Aging Information Center (www.aoa.gov)

WebMD (www.webmd.com)—General medical site with definitions of medical terms and information on diseases and available treatments

Well Spouse Foundation (www.wellspouse.org or 800-838-0879)

Appendix C

Documents and Information to Locate

- Wills/Power of attorney/Healthcare POA—need attorney names, phone numbers, and locations of documents
- Investment statements—a list of assets, location of assets (with account numbers), contact person(s), and phone number(s)
- Credit bureau reports—necessary for the prevention of ID theft and to determine if credit has been damaged
- Net worth statement—the list of all assets, both tangible and intangible
- Life insurance policies—account numbers, location, names, and phone numbers
- Disability insurance policies—same as above
- Long-term care policy—same as above
- Homeowners' insurance—same as above
- Automobile deeds, keys, and bill of sale
- Automobile insurance—policy and account numbers
- Friends and other associates of your parents—people to notify upon the death of your parent(s)

- Last wishes—specific requests regarding funeral, burial, donations, and so on
- Real estate documents

Appendix D

Sample Wish List Spreadsheet

(hypothetical appraised values)

Person	Item	Appraised Value	Duplicate wishes?	With whom?
Karen	Mantel clock	$200	NO	
	Silver bell collection	$250	NO	
	Painting in Mom's room	$375	NO	
	Painting in spare room	$175	NO	
	Rooster statue in kitchen	$25	NO	
	Mom's perfume bottles	$150	NO	
	Antique school desk	$35	NO	
	Mom's childhood doll	$75	NO	
	Grandma's wedding quilt	$375	NO	
	Sterling silver flatware	$1,700	NO	
	Centerpiece in dining room	$45	NO	
	Gold curio cabinet in living room	$225	NO	
	Chandelier, crystal, and brass	$1,500	YES	Jimmy
	Grandfather's tall case clock	$9,000	YES	Jimmy
	Four-gallon pottery churn	$175	NO	
	Mom's diamond earrings	$850	NO	
	Antique fireplace screen	$695	YES	Jimmy
	Karen's TOTAL	$15,850		

Appendix D

Person	Item	Appraised Value	Duplicate wishes?	With whom?
Jimmy	Grandfather's pocket watch	$175	NO	
	Power tools in garage	$250	NO	
	Grandfather's oak rolltop desk	$1,200	NO	
	Dad's pipe collection on stand	$55	NO	
	Dad's letter opener	$15	NO	
	Dining room table and chairs	$1,000	YES	Karen
	La-Z-Boy chair in den	$250	NO	
	Bronze eagle statue on Dad's desk	$375	NO	
	John Deere garden tractor	$2,100	NO	
	Jimmy's TOTAL	$5,420		

Notes

Introduction: Leaving Behind More Than Memories

1. The annual death rate among persons sixty-five and older is approximately 1,756,000. So assuming that the majority of these elderly are parents, one could deduce that each day, forty-eight hundred boomers lose a parent. Death statistics available at the U.S. Centers for Disease Control and Prevention's National Center for Health Statistics, www.cdc.gov/nchs/deaths.htm.

2. John J. Havens and Paul G. Schervick, "Millionaires and the Millennium," Planned Giving Design Center, www.pgdc.com/usa/item/?itemID=26096&gl1n.enc=ISO-8859-1.

Chapter 2: Planning for the Inevitable

1. Psalm 90:10 KJV.

Chapter 3: Where's the Will?

1. "Majority of American Adults Remain Without Wills, New Lawyers. comSM Survey Finds," LexisNexis Media Relations press release, April 3, 2007, www.lexisnexis.com/about/releases/0966.asp.

Chapter 4: When Reality Sinks In

1. For more information about privacy restrictions in the Health Insurance Portability and Accountability Act of 1996 (HIPAA), see www.hipaa.org.

Chapter 5: The Hearse Doesn't Have a Trailer Hitch

1. From Nancy Kershaw, professor of 4-H Development and Family and Community Development, Oregon State University, in a presentation titled "'De-Clutter' Your Life," January 2007. Available at http://extension.oregonstate.edu/fcd/vprograms/fcelessons/fcepdffiles/FCD07-01declutterleaderguide.pdf.

2. Self Storage Association, "Self Storage Industry Fact Sheet," April 19, 2007. Available at www.selfstorage.org/pdf/FactSheet.pdf.

Chapter 7: Scammers, Schemers, and Other Scoundrels

1. National Center of Elder Abuse at the American Public Human Services Association in collaboration with Westat, Inc., "National Elder Abuse Incidence Study," prepared for the Administration for Children and Families and the Administration on Aging in the U.S. Department of Health and Human Services, September 1998. Available at http://www.aoa.gov/eldfam/Elder_Rights/Elder_Abuse/ABuseReport_Full.pdf.

2. Ibid.

3. Christopher Cox, Chairman of the U.S. Securities and Exchange Commission, "Protecting Senior Citizens from Investment Fraud," presented to the U.S. Senate Special Committee on Aging, September 5, 2007. Available at www.sec.gov/news/testimony/2007/ts090507cc.htm.

Chapter 8: The Nitty-Gritty of Dividing Your Parents' Estate

1. National Center of Elder Abuse at the American Public Human Services Association in collaboration with Westat, Inc., "National Elder Abuse Incidence Study," prepared for the Administration for Children and Families and the Administration on Aging in the U.S. Department of Health and Human Services, September 1998. Available at http://www.aoa.gov/eldfam/Elder_Rights/Elder_Abuse/ABuseReport_Full.pdf.

Chapter 12: Right, Wrong, and In Between

1. Larry Colero, "A Framework for Universal Principles of Ethics" (University of British Columbia Center for Applied Ethics), www.ethics.ubc.ca/papers/invited/colero.html.

2. Matthew 7:12; author's paraphrase.

Chapter 14: Be Good to Yourself

1. John Lennon and Paul McCartney, "A Little Help from My Friends," © 1967, Sony/ATV Tunes LLC/Beatles.ASCAP. All rights reserved.

2. Thomas H. Johnson, ed., *The Letters of Emily Dickinson* (Cambridge, MA: Belknap Press, 1958), letter #193, to Samuel Bowles, August 1858 or 1859.

3. Ecclesiastes 4:9 NKJV.

4. Karl Shapiro, "Nostalgia," *New and Selected Poems, 1940–1986* (Chicago: University of Chicago Press, 1987).

5. Norman Cousins describes his experiment in healing himself through laughter in the landmark book, *Anatomy of an Illness* (New York: W.W. Norton, 2005).

Chapter 15: Mission Accomplished!

1. As told to me by family friend, Lyn Cryderman, with the permission of Dr. Kenneth Taylor's estate.

About the Author

Julie Hall is a certified personal property appraiser, estate sales professional, residential content removal specialist, and a broker of fine items. As owner and operator of The Estate Lady®, LLC, which offers turnkey estate dissolution services, she brings seventeen years of experience to families facing the overwhelming task of estate liquidation. Her expertise is called upon for consulting, conducting on-site estate sales, appraising personal property, and organizing the removal and disposal of contents in the most appropriate way.

In addition to her responsibilities as The Estate Lady®, Julie's passion for helping as many distressed families as possible deal with the challenges of estate dissolution inspired her to take ownership of the American Society of Estate Liquidators (ASEL) in 2007. As director of ASEL, her vision is to dedicate the organization to being an educational, networking, and referral resource to estate liquidation professionals nationwide.

A popular speaker to groups dealing with older adult issues and estate accumulation challenges, she has also written a monthly column, "Ask the Estate Lady," to provide answers about appraisals, downsizing, and family matters. Her articles have appeared in newspapers, trade journals, and magazines that target seniors. To help train others, she has developed a course titled "How to Identify Valuables in Your Home or Attic" that she teaches to various groups and organizations.

Julie is a member of the Certified Appraisers Guild of America, the

National Speakers Association, the National Association of Women Business Owners, and the Better Business Bureau. In 2007 The Estate Lady®, LLC was selected by StartupNation as one of the top three home-based businesses in the United States in its Boomers Back in Business category. Julie is also currently pursuing a certificate in appraisal studies in arts and antiques at the Rhode Island School of Design.

Julie resides in Charlotte, North Carolina, with her husband and their daughter. For more information, please visit Julie's Web site:

www.theestatelady.com.